The I ♥ TRADER JOE'S® Cookbook

 *Cherie Mercer Twohy*

More than 150 Delicious Recipes Using Only Foods from the World's Greatest Grocery Store

Ulysses Press

Published by
Ulysses Press
P.O. Box 3440
Berkeley, CA 94703
www.ulyssespress.com

ISBN: 978-1-56975-717-8
Library of Congress Catalog Number 2009902008

Printed in Canada by Transcontinental Printing

10 9 8 7

Acquisitions Editor: Nick Denton-Brown
Managing Editor: Claire Chun
Editors: Teresa Castle, Lauren Harrison
Proofreader: Kate Kellogg
Production: Judith Metzener
Design: what!design @ whatweb.com
Cover photos: front hula dancer © istockphoto.com/dalton00; back food photos © Kevin Twohy
Interior photos: pages 12, 25, 31, 36, 48, 62, 75, 85, 93, 98, 109, 118, 126, 131, 135, 145, 148, 159, 162, 165, 171, 181, 192, 197 © Kevin Twohy; page 10 © Shutterstock.com/Yellowj; page 34 © Shutterstock.com/Cameramannz; page 56 © Shutterstock.com/Krzysztof Slusarczyk; page 60 © Shutterstock.com/Al Mueller; page 71 © Shutterstock.com/Valentyn Volkov; page 81 © Shutterstock.com/Elena Kalistratova; page 88 © Shutterstock.com/Daniel Wiedemann; page 101 © Shutterstock.com/Sandi; page 106 © Shutterstock.com/Tobik; page 121 © Shutterstock.com/LockStockBob; page 122 © Shutterstock.com/Vuk Adzic; page 133 © Shutterstock.com/Barbara J. Petrick; page 139 © Shutterstock.com/Beat Bieler; page 146 © Shutterstock.com/yamix; page 151 © istockphoto.com/AlesVeluscek; page 161 © Shutterstock.com/XuRa; page 166 © Shutterstock.com/Alex Staroseltsev; page 175 © Shutterstock.com/creativeye97; page 182 © Shutterstock.com/Elena Kalistratova; page 191 © Shutterstock.com/Liv frills; page 203 © Shutterstock.com/Fine Shinne; page 205 © Shutterstock.com/Lasse Kristensen; page 217 © Shutterstock.com/carolgaranda

Distributed by Publishers Group West

NOTE TO READERS: TRADER JOE'S® is a registered trademark of Trader Joe's® Company and is used here for informational purposes only. This book is independently authored and published and is not sponsored or endorsed by, or affiliated in any way with, Trader Joe's® Company.

TABLE OF CONTENTS

ACKNOWLEDGMENTS iv

INTRODUCTION 1

STARTERS, SMALL PLATES, NIBBLES, AND NOSHES 9

SALADS 28

SOUP 46

BEANS, RICE, GRAINS, AND POTATOES 59

POULTRY 76

BEEF AND LAMB 90

PORK 105

SEAFOOD 124

PASTA 137

VEGETABLES 156

DESSERTS 178

APPENDIX 207

RECIPE INDEX 214

INGREDIENT INDEX 217

ABOUT THE AUTHOR 220

ACKNOWLEDGMENTS

Thank goodness Trader Joe's has a great array of flowers, because I've got a lot of people to thank!

A bountiful bouquet to the folks at Ulysses Press—Nick Denton-Brown, who found me by Googling, Lauren Harrison, who took the reins partway down the trail, Claire Chun, who skillfully managed the fascinating process of building a book, and Teresa Castle, whose gentle editing suggestions and humor made the process of revision less painful and the book all the better!

Armfuls of sunflowers to Joe's everywhere—the ones I know by name and the ones I've yet to meet. Your sunny smiles and helpful manner make shopping in your stores an enjoyable part of so many people's day. Thanks for your energy and enthusiasm, as well as for stocking those shelves with great stuff every day! In particular, a gorgeous tropical orchid to one specific Joe—the big kahuna—Joe Coulombe, who had the vision.

Long-stemmed roses to the thousands of students who've come through the doors of Chez Cherie over the years. You encourage and inspire me to explore new techniques and flavors for classes. Many of you have become friends, and you are the reason this book was written. Thank you all for your loyalty and support.

A gigantic bundle of mixed blooms to my amazing, supportive, creative, talented, and loving staff. Without Chris Delgado, GeGe Engwald-Parry, Whitnee Haston, Valerie Barth, and Kareen Rowe, the doors of Chez Cherie would not open each week. They are wonderful women-in-food, and I'm so lucky to have them working beside me. And to all of our high-school dishwashers over the years—thanks for your hours in the suds! I hope we repaid you well in spending money *and* in good food!

A rainbow of tulips to the tremendous friends whose support and friendship make life sweet. So many friends to thank, and I'm terrified to leave any out—the "Vigberts," the Murrays, the Salters, and many more…if you've ever raised a glass (or more) of wine at Chez Cherie after hours, please consider yourself thanked here for your love and laughter.

Masses of fragrant blossoms for my family. For my mom, Jane, who never forced me to learn how to cook (despite her sister's claims that I'd never learn…), but encouraged me at whatever I tried. To Steve, my husband of nearly thirty years, who has only cooked for me twice but has willingly tested thousands of recipes with honest reactions. And to my kids—Matt, Kevin, and Brenna, my reasons for being. Having your feet under my table has been the biggest blessing of my life, and I'm so lucky to have gotten you in the "kid lottery."

INTRODUCTION

Before I owned a cooking school, whenever I had friends over for drinks or dinner, they'd ask me, "Where did you get this fabulous cheese?" or, "What's that great spread?" Almost always, the answer included the magic words "Trader Joe's." This happened so frequently that friends even started asking to go to Trader Joe's with me because they had trouble finding the great stuff I loved. It was a bit embarrassing. After all, I did spend a couple years in culinary school. Nevertheless, many of the recipes that turned heads seemed to originate at the same store.

Once I opened Chez Cherie cooking school, I started offering classes featuring Trader Joe's products. I even asked our local store Captain if he'd come spend a few minutes answering students' questions about how the stores select products, how they keep the prices so low, and how they can sell that wine for two bucks! The classes quickly took off, and nine years and four Captains later, they're still among our most popular offerings. I'm always surprised to see how far students have traveled to attend class! That tells me there is a lot of interest in the stores and their products. Of course, I like to think that even though we're not affiliated with them, we're doing some positive outreach for Trader Joe's in the process, since we truly love what they do and appreciate all their great products and prices.

I've always been a huge fan of all the great stuff at Trader Joe's, so preparing for the classes is such fun. Because I am in my local TJ's nearly every day, shopping for my family or for the evening's cooking class (yes, I get most of the ingredients for classes other than our Trader Joe's classes there, too), I tend to get tunnel vision. Let's face it, there is a lot going on in those stores! The aisles are sometimes narrow, the signage is wild and crazy, and the shelves are tightly stocked with colorful packaging. Especially when time is tight, I think we all tend to zero in on the ingredients we need right away and filter out all the other stuff. But the other stuff is such fun! It's great to go to the stores when you aren't in a hurry and just stroll the aisles looking at what's interesting, new, and delicious. There's always a new product to try, especially at the demo stations, where cheerful crew members (I call 'em my "Joes") dish out tasty samples of new products and old favorites all day long. You can get some good ideas for quick and easy dinners by watching those demo darlings. If you have your kids in tow, let them judge whether the samples get a thumbs-up. They seem to be drawn like honeybees to that sample-station counter, and if something catches their fancy, they'll be likely to enjoy it at home, too. It's great to have a product "road tested," especially with finicky eaters.

I'm such a fan of Joe's that I visit three locations regularly. In fact, I find it helps get me inspired to visit a different TJ's store from time to time because the layout is always a little different from my home Joe's. This forces me to look with new eyes, and I tend to notice items I haven't seen before. Since I love to play with ingredients, this is great inspiration for creating menus for classes and for home! Try hitting up a new Joe's when you are in a different neck of the woods. Heck—I even head there when I'm on vacation! Who has better beach or poolside snacks than Trader Joe's? And after-ski or hiking munchables? I may just have to put together a tour of all 300-plus TJ's locations. Road trip!

When I was approached to write this cookbook, I was thrilled, of course, but it also seemed like a daunting task. After all, different Trader Joe's stores carry different items; there are regional and seasonal differences; and things do tend to go in and out of stock. Also, I didn't want to do a cookbook that consisted of "Open carton A, stir in contents of package B." I acknowledge that in our busy lives there is a time and place for that kind of food. I also think that the Trader Joe's cartons and packages are filled with better ingredients and fewer additives, preservatives, and artificial ingredients than those at most other stores. But I wanted us to really cook together. After all, I have a cooking school. Teaching folks to cook is what I love. So, while you will find some very simple, stir-together recipes in this book, there are more ideas for actual cooking than for heating up a Trader Joe's pizza. Sure, those pizzas can be great, but even though we may not have met, I have full confidence in your ability to read the package directions and complete that task successfully.

My hope for this book is that it will serve as inspiration and that the recipes will be jumping-off points for your own brilliant ideas on what to do with that terrific stuff at our favorite place to shop. Please view these recipes as templates, and let your imagination and taste buds suggest other flavor pairings for that rice dish or those palmiers. After all, new products are arriving at your Joe's every week. I'd love to hear your versions of these dishes, and I'm sure I'll be inspired by your changes and additions. You can brag to me at cherie@ilovetraderjoes.com. In the meantime, c'mon, let's go to Joe's!

HOW DO I LOVE THEE, JOE?
LET ME COUNT THE WAYS:

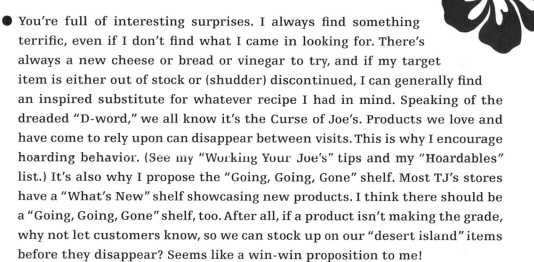

- You're full of interesting surprises. I always find something terrific, even if I don't find what I came in looking for. There's always a new cheese or bread or vinegar to try, and if my target item is either out of stock or (shudder) discontinued, I can generally find an inspired substitute for whatever recipe I had in mind. Speaking of the dreaded "D-word," we all know it's the Curse of Joe's. Products we love and have come to rely upon can disappear between visits. This is why I encourage hoarding behavior. (See my "Working Your Joe's" tips and my "Hoardables" list.) It's also why I propose the "Going, Going, Gone" shelf. Most TJ's stores have a "What's New" shelf showcasing new products. I think there should be a "Going, Going, Gone" shelf, too. After all, if a product isn't making the grade, why not let customers know, so we can stock up on our "desert island" items before they disappear? Seems like a win-win proposition to me!

- You hire people who seem to be happy to work for you. I really appreciate that positive spirit these days, when "customer service" has to be put in quotation marks and pronounced with an ironically arched brow. From what I've gleaned, you treat them well, which is part of the reason they whistle while they work. (It could also be those Muzak melodies wafting through the aisles—I confess that the Beach Boys tunes occasionally have me pushing my cart to the tempo!—but most of the folks in the hibiscus-patterned T-shirts are far too young to recognize those oldies.) I enjoy shopping in a place where I'm greeted with a genuine smile and where, if I ask for help, someone will put down the box cutter and gently guide me to the correct area of the store.

- Your stores are interesting in ways that grocery stores and big box stores are not. You employ actual human artists at each store to create colorful murals, signs, and other artwork that make each location unique. I like noticing that the store in La Crescenta looks different the Ventura store.

- You have a "mom 'n' pop" attitude, even though you aren't a mom 'n' pop store. You foster community engagement through your Captains, and your stores frequently donate bottled water for fund-raising 5K runs or other local good works. Your crew members will go the extra mile, whether it's helping an overloaded shopper to the car or offering crazy TJ's stickers to a tired toddler. Both gestures are small, but at the right moment, they can make the difference between a good day and a meltdown.

- Your prices are fair, or more than fair, and your return and exchange policies couldn't be more egalitarian. Basically, it boils down to, "If you don't like it, bring it back, and we'll make it right." I appreciate that I can feel free to try something new, knowing that if it doesn't suit my palate, I can exchange it for something I'll love. And, of course, knowing that makes me a much more adventurous shopper.

- Your products are not full of preservatives, additives, and things I can't pronounce. Yes, sometimes that means a loaf of bread may begin to "sprout" after a few days on my counter. I can live with that. I'm scared of bread that doesn't sprout or go stale because there are probably lots of things in there that I don't want to eat.

- You educate me with brochures and labeling on gluten-free, vegetarian and vegan, kosher, and all manner of dietary disciplines. I'm sure I'd appreciate this even more if I adhered to one of those diets, but even though I don't, the information is interesting and informative.

- You don't have a loyalty program or three-day sales. (Why do I always show up at my grocery store on the wrong day for those?) Instead, you keep the prices low every day, and I get the feeling that you and I are loyal to one another without having to fumble for that plastic key fob or membership card!

- You make it easy to check the "What's New" shelf or grab a sample of something at the demo stations. The fact that I may find a new favorite product keeps me fighting for a parking space in your lot and takes a little bit of the sting away when something I love disappears from the shelves.

- Your outdoor floral displays brighten my day, even if I'm not buying blossoms. Way to decorate the cart corral!

● You provide a great mix of ready-to-eat meals and ready-to-cook ingredients. Some days just don't lend themselves to donning an apron and preheating the oven. Other times, nothing will do but getting a big pot of soup simmering on the stovetop. I appreciate that you equip me for both!

WORKING YOUR JOE'S: STRATEGIES FOR GETTING THE BEST OUT OF YOUR TRADER JOE'S® EXPERIENCE

● MAKE FRIENDS WITH YOUR "JOES." It's easy to do because they are friendly by nature. When I visit a TJ's, I often pay attention to the crew, and they are nearly always smiling, chatting, and offering help. Frequently, I'll pass a crew member in the aisle, and he or she will ask, "Can I help you find something?" (Not sure whether I look particularly helpless, but it's still nice.) I have overheard crew members deftly handle some very difficult customers with aplomb; they really do aim to please. Once you've established a relationship, your friends at TJ's will alert you to new stuff they think you might like. If you need something in quantity, call ahead, and they'll set it aside for you— not that they wouldn't do that anyway, but it's just more like dealing with a mom 'n' pop merchant if you are on a first-name basis.

● CHECK OUT THE WEBSITE. There's been a terrific improvement in the Trader Joe's website in the past few years: tons of dietary information, new product blurbs, and even recipes. (Hey! That's my job!) If there's a recall on an item, you can read about it not only at the checkout counter, where signs are posted, but also on the website. You can also read about TJ's lore, find store locations, and even talk back to Joe! E-mail your questions or fill TJ's in on your joys (at a new product that has rocked your world) or sorrows (I can't live much longer without the Hot and Sweet Mustard!). I've been told by Trader Joe's insiders that they do take customer requests very seriously, so let 'em know what you're thinking.

● HOARD YOUR FAVORITES. Hoarding is an ugly word, but sometimes ya gotta. Most of us have experienced the Heartbreak of TJ's when that staple ingredient, be it mustard, pie crust, or a particularly delicious mojito sauce, suddenly disappears from the shelf, leaving devoted customers feeling bereft. I've been shopping at Trader Joe's so long that I've been down this Heartbreak Road many, many times. So now, when I find some new shelf-stable or freezable item that I fall in love with, I purchase two or three. I use those and replace them as I do, so I've always got a couple in reserve in case there's a supply problem and my TJ's is out for a week or two. I also watch the shelves for signs of change. If my favorite salsa usually has a "four-jar-across" placement and I notice that it has diminished to two, I get nervous. I'll see if I can find out why it's in short supply, and if I can't, I'll grab a few extra jars, just in case.

- **GO TO "THE ALTAR."** The folks up there *know stuff.* Rather than ask a crew member who's stocking shelves about a product, head up to the front desk and ask someone there. They have access to a computer list that will give you the straight scoop on whether something is held up at a port of entry (which happened during the Great Caper Shortage of '08), or TOS (temporarily out of stock), or the dreaded DISCONTINUED. If something you love and need has been (horrors!) given the big "D" (and it *is* a sort of divorce, sometimes—painful and sudden, and you feel helpless and alone), ask for the flier that contains addresses and phone numbers for all the TJ's locations. Zero in on the ones in your "willing to drive there" zone and call them. (I am a little embarrassed to admit that I have more than two TJ's on my speed dial.) If they have some of your beloved item in stock, they'll hold it for you. Me? I'm not a "cold turkey" kind of girl. I need to wean myself from my current favorite pasta shape or vinegar. So I grab what I can, and each time I open a package, I remind myself that this is nearly the end of this particular love affair and soon it will be time to move on to another great product.

- **THINK OUTSIDE THE FROZEN-FOOD BOX.** Just because it says frozen carrots doesn't mean you can't use it in a million ways. Think about the ingredient, not the finished product. Don't look at that frozen brown rice just as a microwavable side dish—think of it as a head start on fried rice (using up the remnants of several bags of frozen veggies and the last egg in the carton), or as an add-in to make leftover soup heartier and more healthful.

- **WATCH THE DISPLAYS FOR NEW ITEMS AND "HUSTLE BUYS."** This is a good way to find a great new snack or salad dressing or grab a terrific bottle of Hustle Buy wine or beer at a fantastic price before it's going-going-gone.

- **LISTEN TO OTHER CUSTOMERS AND ASK QUESTIONS.** Trader Joe's is a friendly place, so they will probably be happy to help. If you see someone putting eight boxes of curry sauce in her cart, ask what fabulous dish she has in mind. Not only will you get a great recipe idea, you might also make a friend. After all, you have a discerning appreciation of Trader Joe's in common.

WHAT TO DO IN A PINCH:
TIPS ON SUBSTITUTING INGREDIENTS

While writing this book, I've assumed that folks who are cooking from this book either shop regularly at Trader Joe's, have a TJ's nearby, or have at least had the pleasure of visiting one of these terrific stores once or twice. After all, every single ingredient in this book is carried there. But because they occasionally run out of an item, or, sadly, discontinue them, or because you may have plucked this book from the shelf at a vacation house far from a Trader Joe's, some substitution suggestions might be helpful.

I've attempted to give sizes for any containers of products called for, so that you have an idea of how much of an ingredient you'll need if, for example Trader Joe's Corn and Chile Tomato-Less Salsa is not currently available to you. In that case, you'll know how much of another brand to substitute. While I'm a firm believer in the TJ's brands, I know there may be times when you can't reach one to get their great stuff. After all, they are currently in only half of our fifty states! (By the way, if you *do* need a substitute for that corn salsa, use about 1½ cups fresh or frozen corn kernels; a chopped jalapeño or about a tablespoon of canned, chopped chiles; and a splash of vinegar. Or just use the corn and about a half cup of prepared salsa. It won't be the real deal, but you'll get by.)

SO HERE ARE SOME TIPS ON EASY SUBSTITUTIONS:

- Where cubes of frozen garlic are called for, a cube is close to a clove of minced garlic, which is also about a teaspoonful.

- Crème fraîche and heavy cream can be used interchangeably in these recipes with satisfactory results. In a pinch, sour cream can usually be substituted for crème fraîche, but since sour cream is not as heat-stable, use care when adding cold sour cream to a hot sauce, as the sour cream may break, causing a curdled appearance.

- If mascarpone is not available, cream cheese is an acceptable, if less flavorful, alternative. Use the block form, not whipped, for the most accurate measurement.

- Tabasco (my fave is Tabasco with Chipotle), Cholula, Crystal, or other good-quality hot sauces can be used in place of the TJ's brands.

- While I've never found any equal in quality to Trader Joe's pie dough, there are other brands of ready-made and rolled pie dough and puff pastry, and they'll do in a pinch. I think using them will only renew an allegiance to the Trader Joe's products in the future. The TJ's frozen pie dough is currently stocked seasonally, as is the frozen puff pastry. Believe me when I tell you that you cannot have too many boxes of either item in your freezer. So, in winter, clear out your freezer and fill it with these two great products. *I think pie season is year-round, but until Trader Joe's carries these products in all seasons, you'll need to hoard!*

- Bagged salad mixes can be used interchangeably in these recipes. If you love a different Trader Joe's blend than I've called for, use that one. And if you are far from a Joe's, I've given sizes in ounces so you can pick up an appropriately sized bag, plus or minus an ounce or so.

- When it comes to broth, the best substitute is homemade broth, and if you do that, you are a kitchen rock star. If you're using a commercial broth, try to use a low-sodium brand that's not canned because I think there's some flavor transfer from the can. I'm a big fan of Penzeys spices (www.penzeys.com), and they have wonderful broth concentrates.

- If you are looking for a substitute for a particular tapenade that I've mentioned, just look for something with a similar flavor profile to the one I've specified and go for it! That's how recipes are created!

- If Rice Sticks are not available (they are stocked regionally), you can usually find them in a grocery store with a good selection of Asian products, or just use a long pasta like linguine.

Most other ingredient substitutions will be obvious—another brand of cooked sausage, another gingerbread mix, another frozen vegetable. Play with these recipes—they're printed, not chiseled. And I'd love to hear from you if you either run aground or hit on something amazing! I can be reached at cherie@ilovetraderjoes.com.

See you at TJ's!

Chapter 1

STARTERS, SMALL PLATES, NIBBLES, AND NOSHES

Personally, I could live on a steady diet of snacks from Trader Joe's! Crackers and cheeses alone would sustain me for weeks. Then there are the spreads, dips, and a rainbow of hummuses (hummi?) to liven up anything from crudités to pitas.

The nut section is jammed with fresh and interesting blends, spiced and candied nuts, and all manner of trail mixes and dried fruits. One of the many things I love about TJ's is that the nut section has such quick turnover. That's important, because nuts are full of oil, which makes them taste great, but it also means they can go rancid pretty quickly. A rancid nut is not a pretty thing. For that reason, I always try to buy nuts where the turnover is high so I know that the nuts are fresh and haven't been sitting on the shelf all season. I store nuts in the freezer so they stay fresh longer and then toast them in a dry sauté pan to reactivate those flavorful oils before use.

One of my hands-down favorite TJ's items of the past few years is the utterly fabulous frozen Artisan Puff Pastry. Why do I love it so much? For one thing, it's flat, not folded like a letter. This makes much more sense for puff pastry, because the cracks that inevitably ensue when you unfold it are not as easily repaired as with, say, pie crust. Also, it's made with butter instead of hydrolyzed what-have-you. Let's face it—puff pastry is not a health food, so I say go for the glorious taste and texture that butter brings to the party, and diet tomorrow. This puff pastry is better than any commercial pastry I've ever found, and even better than puff pastry I made myself, from scratch, back in my overachieving culinary-school days. Pick a spread or tapenade off the shelf, slather it on a sheet of defrosted puff, roll or cut the pastry into serving sizes, bake it, and you're almost guaranteed a winning appetizer. Toss a handful of cheese or chopped nuts on there, and you're a culinary genius. I get really nervous if I have fewer than five boxes of this frozen treasure on hand. The frozen puff pastry is stocked seasonally, so my advice is to seriously hoard the stuff. If they ever discontinue this … well, I simply can't contemplate that tragedy.

From simple to stellar, the recipes in this section are designed to get your creative juices flowing (and your mouth watering). Making a meal of appetizers, tapas-style, is my favorite way to eat and also to entertain. Whether you are making one quick nibble or an impressive array of hors d'oeuvres, I hope you'll add these to your repertoire.

WARM ALMONDS and OLIVES

The glistening olives and brown-skinned almonds look gorgeously rustic. And a 10-minute tapa is always a good thing! Pop a bottle of Cava and, by the time you've had a few sips, these fragrant nibbles will be ready to munch. Their aroma will have you pressing your nose against the oven window!

2 (10-ounce) containers Trader Joe's Greek Olive Medley, drained

1 cup dry-roasted (salted or unsalted) almonds

3 tablespoons olive oil

several long swaths of orange and/or lemon peel (removed with a vegetable peeler or channel knife)

several sprigs of rosemary

VEGETARIAN, VEGAN, GLUTEN-FREE

Preheat oven to 375°F. In an ovenproof baking dish, combine the olives, almonds, olive oil, and all but one of the orange or lemon peel swaths and rosemary sprigs. Place the baking dish in the oven and heat until warm, 10 to 15 minutes. If the citrus peel and rosemary look too charred, replace with the reserved ones. Serve with bread for dipping in the olive oil after the olives and almonds are gone.

Serves: 4 to 6

Prep Time: 5 minutes

Cooking Time: 10 to 15 minutes

. . . .

This is a recipe in which the oven temperature really doesn't matter—if you have the oven on for something else, just pop the baking dish in and adjust the time to the temperature. All you're doing is warming stuff up!

. . . .

CHERRY CROSTINI with PECORINO ROMANO

So simple, so pretty, so unusual. What more do you need from a 10-minute appetizer? The Trader Joe's Cherry Preserves are marvelously chunky, which is perfect for these little bites of wonderful.

1 loaf of artisan-style bread (I love the Trader Joe's Organic Whole Grain Loaf)

1 (17.5-ounce) jar Trader Joe's Cherry Preserves

freshly ground black pepper

Pecorino Romano cheese, for garnish

VEGETARIAN

Preheat oven to 400°F or use a toaster oven. Slice the bread into ¼-inch slices. Spread each slice with some of the cherry preserves. Generously season with black pepper. Place on a baking sheet and warm in the oven, 4 to 6 minutes. Using a vegetable peeler, shave several swaths of Pecorino Romano over the warm crostini.

Serves: About 20 servings per loaf

Prep Time: 5 minutes

Cooking Time: 5 minutes

Try some toasted and chopped walnuts or pine nuts sprinkled on top.

ROASTED APRICOTS *with* HONEYED GOAT CHEESE

 *At Chez Cherie, we've used this recipe in several Aphrodisia cooking classes. Sexy and delicious, the soft flesh of the apricot pairs beautifully with the tangy cheese. The whisper of heat from the hot sauce should induce a very slight lip tingle.*

4 lusciously ripe apricots, halved and pitted (if apricots are not in season, use plump, plush dried ones)

4 ounces soft, fresh goat cheese, such as Trader Joe's Chèvre, Madame Chèvre, or Silver Goat Chèvre

small splash of Trader Joe's Chili Pepper Hot Sauce or Jalapeño Pepper Hot Sauce

2 tablespoons honey

1 tablespoon pistachios, coarsely chopped

VEGETARIAN, GLUTEN-FREE

Preheat broiler. Fill the hollows of the apricots with mounds of goat cheese. Arrange on a baking sheet and place under broiler for 2 to 3 minutes, until slightly browned. Remove from heat. Stir a drop or two of the hot sauce into the honey and drizzle the spiked honey over the apricots. Sprinkle with chopped pistachios.

Serves: 4
Prep Time: 5 minutes
Cooking Time: 3 minutes

TSAO NUTS

These spicy-sweet beauties are great in salads, as a garnish for savory dishes, or to simply gobble by the handful!

⅓ cup Trader Joe's General Tsao
Stir-Fry Sauce

2 tablespoons honey

2 cups pecans

freshly ground black pepper

VEGETARIAN

Preheat oven to 300°F. Line a baking sheet with a silicone baking mat or parchment. In a large bowl, mix the General Tsao sauce and honey and then stir in the pecans to coat well. Arrange in a single layer on the lined baking sheet and bake, stirring once or twice, for 35 to 45 minutes, until nuts are well-coated and sauce has formed a glaze. Remove from the oven and sprinkle with freshly ground black pepper. Cool slightly before removing from baking sheet, and break into pieces.

Makes: 2 cups

Prep Time: less than 5 minutes

Cooking Time: 45 minutes or less

If you like things extra-spicy, you can use some crushed red chile pepper flakes along with the black pepper, but take it easy! These spicy morsels are great for munching or for garnishing a salad.

MATT'S MAGIC MUSHROOMS

My oldest son, Matt, is a professional cook. (Could I be any prouder?) When he was a teenager, he improvised this recipe from one he saw online. My catering friends have used it for years. I think they owe Matt some royalties!

4 strips Niman Ranch Applewood Smoked Dry-Cured Bacon

12 Trader Joe's Stuffing Portabella Mushrooms (2 packages)

2 shallots, minced

2 cubes frozen crushed garlic

1 cup packed baby spinach leaves

2 ounces (about ⅓ cup) feta cheese

2 ounces mascarpone or cream cheese

pinch of red chile pepper flakes

salt and pepper

GLUTEN-FREE

Preheat oven to 400°F. Line a baking sheet with parchment. In a medium sauté pan, cook the bacon over medium-high heat until crisp, about 8 minutes. Remove bacon to a paper towel to drain. Pour all but a tablespoon of the bacon fat into a heatproof container and reserve. Brush the portabella mushrooms on both sides with the reserved bacon fat. You may have to add a little olive oil to coat them thoroughly. Place the rounded side of the mushrooms on the parchment-lined baking sheet and sprinkle with salt and pepper. Bake the mushrooms for 15 minutes, then turn them over and bake for an additional 10 minutes. While they bake, prepare the filling.

FILLING: In the same sauté pan you used to cook the bacon, sauté the shallots and garlic in the 1 tablespoon bacon fat until fragrant and softened, about 5 minutes. Cool to room temperature. Place the spinach in the bowl of a food processor and coarsely chop. Add the bacon and process again. Add the shallot-garlic mixture and pulse to combine, then add the feta and mascarpone or cream cheese and pulse again to combine. Season to taste with salt, pepper, and red chile pepper flakes.

TO ASSEMBLE: Turn the mushrooms rounded side down and spoon a mound of filling into each mushroom cap. Return the mushrooms to the oven and bake until heated through, 5 to 7 minutes.

Serves: 6
Prep Time: 20 minutes
Cooking Time: 30 minutes

Large white mushrooms can be substituted for the portabellas.

ARTICHOKE *and* BASIL SPREAD

This is a really versatile spread. I love to make garlic bread with it, or use it as a pasta sauce or a pizza topping. My favorite "dippers" for this spread are Trader Joe's Lowfat Rye Mini Toasts.

large handful of basil leaves

1 (12-ounce) bag Trader Joe's frozen artichoke hearts, defrosted

2 cubes frozen crushed garlic

¼ cup Greek or Mediterranean plain yogurt

squeeze of lemon juice

pinch of red chile pepper flakes or a shake of hot sauce (to taste)

½ cup grated Parmesan cheese

VEGETARIAN, GLUTEN-FREE

In a food processor, chop the basil leaves roughly. Add the artichoke hearts and garlic cubes and chop coarsely. Add the yogurt, lemon juice, red chile pepper flakes or hot sauce, and Parmesan cheese, and process to desired consistency (chunky or smooth). Adjust seasoning to taste.

Serves: 4 to 6
Prep Time: 5 minutes
Cooking Time: none

THESE LITTLE PIGGIES

Adorable sliders in a flash. Put a platter of these in front of a crowd of sports fans, and they'll disappear faster than a two-point lead. Better make a triple batch.

8 Sesame Seed Pull-Apart Rolls, or other rolls (see note)

1 (18-ounce) container Trader Joe's BBQ Shredded Pork

about ½ cup Trader Joe's Corn and Chile Tomato-Less Salsa

1 ripe avocado

Slice the rolls horizontally and toast them, if desired, in a toaster oven or under the broiler in a regular oven. Heat the pork according to package directions. Pile 2 to 3 tablespoons of the pork on each roll and top with a tablespoon of salsa. Add a slice of avocado and finish with the top of the roll.

Serves: 4
Prep Time: 5 minutes
Cooking Time: 5 minutes

....

If the pull-apart rolls aren't available, use Brioche Buns, Panini Rolls, or Focaccia Rolls, cut into two-bite pieces.

....

BAKED CAMEMBERT with HONEY and HAZELNUTS

A rustic bistro appetizer in the blink of un oeil. *This is a simple but oh-so-French presentation that's perfect for a picnic, even if it's on the coffee table.* Très bon.

1 round (about 250 grams or 9 ounces) Camembert or another creamy, soft cheese in a *stapled wooden box*

2 tablespoons flavorful honey

2 tablespoons chopped hazelnuts (or other nuts)

sliced baguette or crackers, and/ or sliced apples or pears

VEGETARIAN, GLUTEN-FREE
(if gluten-free crackers or fruit are used)

Preheat oven to 350°F. Remove the cheese from the box, unwrap, and cut off the top rind. (Don't throw it away—that's the "cook's treat"!) Place the cheese back in the box, drizzle the honey over the top, and scatter the chopped hazelnuts on top. Place on a baking sheet and bake until cheese is warmed, about 12 to 15 minutes. Serve with baguette or crackers, or sliced fruit.

Serves: 4 (or just me)
Prep Time: 5 minutes
Cooking Time: 15 minutes

....
The Camembert in the adorable wooden box is a holiday item, so if it's not in stock, try this with another creamy cheese. Just put it in a small, ovenproof baking dish.
....

ASPARAGUS, PROVOLONE, and PROSCIUTTO INVOLTINI

 Emily Post grants permission to eat asparagus with one's fingers. By all means, do so with these irresistible treats. The combination of the nutty asparagus, gooey cheese, and salty, rich pork is a winner.

12 asparagus spears, about pencil thickness

6 slices provolone

12 slices prosciutto, speck, or Black Forest ham

GLUTEN-FREE

Preheat oven to 400°F. Trim the stem end of the asparagus, place the spears on a baking sheet, and roast for 6 to 8 minutes, until nearly tender (but not floppy). Remove from oven and cool slightly. Cut each provolone slice in half. Starting with the cut edge, roll a slice of cheese around each asparagus spear. Don't worry if it cracks and breaks a little—the prosciutto will hold everything together. Wind a slice of prosciutto around the cheese-wrapped spear (in a spiral) and place on baking sheet again. Repeat with remaining ingredients. Return the baking sheet to the oven and bake until cheese is slightly melted, about 5 minutes.

Serves: 4 to 6
Prep Time: 15 minutes
Cooking Time: less than 15 minutes

• •

Involtini simply means one thing wrapped inside another. These are also great with the jarred artichokes with stems. Substitute the stemmed beauties for the asparagus—you may want to cut them in half, from tip to stem.

• •

APPLE SAUSAGE and CHEDDAR BITES

Yeah, they're kinda pigs in blankets. But really tasty pigs in wonderful, flaky eiderdowns.

1 sheet Trader Joe's Artisan Puff Pastry, thawed but kept cold

about 2 tablespoons Dijon mustard

½ cup grated sharp cheddar cheese

2 Trader Joe's fully cooked Smoked Apple Chardonnay Chicken Sausages

Preheat oven to 400°F. On a lightly floured board, slightly roll the puff pastry, if necessary, to about ¼-inch thickness. (Roll from the center toward the edges, but try not to "clunk" the rolling pin over the edges, as it will compress the dough and inhibit the flaky layers from puffing.) Cut the pastry in half. Spread a little mustard over the surface of each piece of pastry, leaving the edges clean. Sprinkle half the grated cheese over the surface of the pastry, leaving the edges clean. Place a sausage at one long edge of one of the pieces of pastry and roll up the pastry to encase it completely. Repeat with the second sausage and pastry. Place on a baking sheet and bake until the pastry is golden, about 18 minutes. Cool slightly before cutting into 1-inch pieces with a serrated knife.

Serves: 4
Prep Time: 10 minutes
Cooking Time: less than 20 minutes

Don't limit yourself to one type of sausage with this recipe. TJ's has about a dozen flavors of these precooked flavor bombs, so try the Trader Joe's Sweet Apple Chicken Sausage, or the Smoked Andouille Chicken Sausage, or any of the other great combinations.

GREEN OLIVE
and GORGONZOLA PALMIERS

These crispy treats are great as an appetizer or with a bowl of soup. The Trader Joe's frozen puff pastry is high on my "desert island" list. It's the best puff I've ever worked with, including homemade, which is not something that happens often in my life!

1 sheet Trader Joe's Artisan Puff Pastry, defrosted but kept cold

½ (10-ounce) jar Trader Joe's green Olive Tapenade

½ cup crumbled Gorgonzola (or another easily crumbled, not-too-wet cheese)

VEGETARIAN

Preheat oven to 400°F. On a lightly floured board, slightly roll the puff pastry, if necessary, to about ¼-inch thickness. (Roll from the center toward the edges, but try not to "clunk" the rolling pin over the edges, as it will compress the dough and inhibit the flaky layers from puffing.) Spread the tapenade over the dough, leaving a small border clean on all sides. Scatter the Gorgonzola evenly over the surface, and gently press in with the palms of your hands. Starting with one long edge, roll up the dough fairly tightly in a spiral fashion toward the center. Repeat with the other long edge until the two spirals meet in the center. With a sharp knife or bench scraper, cut crosswise slices about ½-inch thick. Place the palmiers on a parchment-lined baking sheet. If the dough seems soft, chill in freezer 10 minutes. Bake until puffed and golden, about 18 minutes.

Serves: 6
Prep Time: 10 minutes
Cooking Time: less than 20 minutes

• •

There are tons of possibilities here—try the Roasted Red Pepper and Artichoke Tapenade with some grated Parmesan cheese, or the Trader Joe's Eggplant Garlic Spread with a little feta cheese, or maybe the Red Pepper Spread with Eggplant and Garlic. You'll come up with your own terrific flavor-popping creations once you see how easily these come together and what a great "wow" factor they generate!

• •

ROASTED PEAR, PROSCIUTTO, and GOAT CHEESE PARCELS

 So easy, pretty, and fun. A great party appetizer that your guest will enjoy making, too. Pour some glasses of sparkling wine and get the first arrivals to wrap and roll for you!

1 ripe pear (I like Bosc or Anjou), cut in eighths, seeded and cored

2 ounces goat cheese (or blue cheese)

balsamic vinegar for drizzling

8 slices prosciutto or speck

GLUTEN-FREE

Preheat oven to 425°F. Place a scant tablespoon of cheese in the hollow of each pear wedge. Drizzle with a little balsamic vinegar and wrap a slice of prosciutto or speck around each wedge. Place on a baking sheet and roast for 6 to 8 minutes, until pears are warm and beginning to brown.

Serves: 4
Prep Time: 5 minutes
Cooking Time: less than 10 minutes

• •

Speck is a glorious thing, and I'm so glad Trader Joe's started to carry it! Made from a pork leg, smoked with aromatic wood, then cured, this munchable treat is great all by itself, but it's also a versatile ingredient that's sometimes hard to find.

• •

MEATBALL SPIEDINI with OVOLINI

Kids of all ages love these colorful kabobs. They have a polka-dot look that's just pure fun. Carry the dotted theme further by halving some large tomatoes, placing them cut-side-down on a platter, and sticking the skewers in for display. You can scatter extra cherry tomatoes and mozzarella balls on the plate, too.

1 (20-ounce) bag Trader Joe's Party Size Mini Meatballs, thawed or still frozen

1 (25-ounce) jar Trader Giotto's Organic Vodka Pasta Sauce (or another tasty pasta sauce)

about 40 fresh basil leaves, rinsed

1 (16-ounce) container Trader Joe's Mixed Medley Cherry Tomatoes or 1 pound heirloom tomatoes, cut in wedges

short bamboo skewers or long toothpicks

1 (8-ounce) container Trader Joe's Ovolini or Ciliegine mozzarella in lightly salted water

GLUTEN-FREE

Simmer the meatballs in the sauce until cooked through (which will take longer if they are still frozen) and coated with sauce. Wrap a basil leaf around a meatball and pierce with a bamboo skewer, securing the basil leaf in place. Top each meatball with a wedge of heirloom tomato or a cherry tomato, a piece of mozzarella, and another tomato. (If you are using the ovolini, cut it in marble-sized pieces.) Finish with another basil leaf. Repeat with remaining ingredients to create more spiedini.

Serves: 4 to 6

Prep Time: 15 minutes

Cooking Time: less than 10 minutes for thawed meatballs, less than 20 for frozen

• •

Spiedini means skewers in Italian. *Ciliegine* means cherry, and it's a great name for these little cherry-sized mozzarella balls. Perfectly shaped for popping in your mouth, they are great for this dish or for scattering in a salad or on a pizza.

• •

ASPARAGUS TART

I loved a clipping of this recipe that I found in the Los Angeles Times *food section about a decade ago. I lost the tattered newsprint version a while back but have been making it by heart ever since. This is a great spring appetizer or brunch dish. You can get very "Type A" and line up all the spears with the points in one direction, or you can do my preferred tumbled look.*

2 teaspoons butter or olive oil

1 onion, thinly sliced

1 sheet Trader Joe's Artisan Puff Pastry, defrosted but kept cool

1 cup grated Gruyère or smoked Gouda

1 (12-ounce) package asparagus

handful of chopped hazelnuts or other nuts (optional)

zest of 1 orange or lemon

VEGETARIAN

Preheat oven to 400°F. In a medium sauté pan, heat the butter or olive oil and sauté the onion over medium-high heat until slightly softened, about 10 minutes. Set aside to cool to room temperature. On a lightly floured board, slightly roll out the puff pastry, if necessary, to about ¼-inch thickness. (Roll from the center toward the edges, but try not to "clunk" the rolling pin over the edges, as it will compress the dough and inhibit the flaky layers from puffing.) Transfer to a parchment-lined baking sheet. Scatter the grated cheese over the pastry, leaving about a ½-inch edge clean on all sides. Fold the pastry up to make a "picture frame" or score the edge with a knife or fork to make it pretty. Top with the sautéed onion. Place the asparagus in a single layer on top, cutting to fit if necessary. Bake until pale golden, about 18 to 20 minutes if not using nuts. If using nuts, scatter them over the surface of the tart after it has baked 15 minutes and return the tart to the oven for about 5 more minutes. Remove from oven and sprinkle the zest over the top. Cut into squares to serve.

Serves: 4 to 6
Prep Time: 15 minutes
Cooking Time: 20 minutes

BRIE and PEAR GALETTE

TJ's pie dough is so good that I know a professional baker who uses it in a pinch. I'm sure she hides the box deep in the recycle bin, so her secret is safe with me! Look for it in the freezer, and since it's not always available, stock up when you see it.

1 Trader Joe's Gourmet Pie Crust, thawed and rolled out to mend any cracks (refreeze the remaining one for another use)

4 ounces Brie (rind removed), cubed

1 pear, thinly sliced

½ cup pecans, coarsely chopped

freshly ground black pepper

VEGETARIAN

Preheat oven to 375°F. Place the pie dough on a baking sheet and scatter half the Brie over the center, leaving the edges clean. Arrange the sliced pears on top of the Brie. Scatter the pecans on top, and then add the remaining Brie. Fold the edges of the dough in to create a "picture frame" around the filling, leaving the center exposed. Grind a little black pepper over the filling and bake 20 to 25 minutes, until crust is golden. Cut into wedges or squares to serve.

Serves: 4 to 6
Prep Time: 10 minutes
Cooking Time: 25 minutes

• •

Try this with Gorgonzola instead of Brie—rather than putting the last half of the cheese on before the galette goes in the oven, reserve it to scatter on top of the galette as soon as it comes out of the oven. Pour a glass of port, and you're in heaven.

• •

CARAMELIZED ONION, FIG, and GORGONZOLA TART

Cut into small squares, this makes a great appetizer. A bigger slice and a glass of red wine, and I'm set for dinner!

1 tablespoon butter

1 red onion, thinly sliced

pinch of sugar

pinch of salt

1 sheet Trader Joe's Artisan Puff Pastry, defrosted but kept cold

handful of dried Mission figs, cut in half (or 2 fresh figs, sliced)

2 tablespoons mascarpone or cream cheese

handful of crumbled Gorgonzola (or other blue cheese)

freshly ground black pepper

VEGETARIAN

In a medium sauté pan, melt the butter. Add the onions, sugar, and salt, and sauté over low heat until soft and caramelized, about 15 minutes. Remove onions from pan and cool to room temperature. Preheat oven to 400°F. On a lightly floured board, slightly roll the puff pastry, if necessary, to about ¼-inch thickness. (Roll from the center toward the edges, but try not to "clunk" the rolling pin over the edges, as it will compress the dough and inhibit the flaky layers from puffing.) Fold about ½ inch of the edges in to make a "picture frame." Spread the room-temperature caramelized onions over the pastry and scatter the figs over the surface. Dot with mascarpone or cream cheese and bake until pastry is golden, about 18 minutes. Scatter the cheese over the tart and season with freshly ground black pepper.

Serves: 4 to 6

Prep Time: about 30 minutes, including cooking the onions, which can be done ahead

Cooking Time: 15 to 20 minutes

Chapter 2

SALADS

J remember waaaay back when TJ's carried very little fresh produce. Now, it's the only place in my neighborhood where I can get mâche, a gorgeous, flowerlike cluster of tender, nutty salad leaves. During the holidays, they even carry pomegranate arils, the ruby-colored seeds inside those leathery casings, which can be murder to remove. When my kids were little, we had a neighbor who liked to "gift" them with these delicious, healthful, but incredibly messy fruits. I would only let them eat the fruit naked, in the bathtub, to avoid indelible stains on T-shirts and under fingernails! So, when I first saw that little jewel box of preseeded glory, I couldn't believe my good fortune! I think I thanked Joe right out loud.

The packaged salads and mixed greens are mostly triple-washed, although I confess to rewashing them myself. I'm not sure I'm eradicating anything with my extra rinse, but it makes me feel proactive, and I think it refreshes the greens at the same time. To ensure the liveliest possible greens, be vigilant about checking expiration dates, and use them within a day or two of purchase.

The oil and vinegar section at TJ's is small but mighty, with an assortment of high-quality olive oils in manageable sizes. Let's face it: it's no bargain to purchase a gallon of olive oil if you use only about a pint a month. Olive oil does not improve with age, and if you use just half of it before it goes rancid, you've wasted the money you meant to save by buying in bulk. Since I live in California and like to eat locally grown products, I love the Trader Joe's California Estate Olive Oil. Why not decrease the food miles and enjoy those delectably oily fruits that are grown in California? This oil is unfiltered and made with Arbequina olives, which have a buttery top note with a hint of pepper at the back of the throat. I especially appreciate the dark-tinted bottle—it filters out some ultraviolet rays, which hasten the spoilage of oils. Another favorite is the Spanish olive oil, which comes packaged in a sexy, square bottle with a cork stopper and a green wax seal. Any time I'm doing tapas, this is my go-to oil.

TJ's generally has a couple of interesting vinegars on the shelf—my current favorite is the Orange Muscat Champagne Vinegar. I mourn the discontinuation of the amazing Pomegranate Vinegar. That stuff was so fragrant, I was always tempted to dab some on my pulse points! Of course, being the TJ hoarder that I am, I have a treasured half bottle in reserve. But Joe, how 'bout bringing that one back? The red wine vinegar is good quality, and their balsamics, though far from the $150-a-bottle elixirs found in gourmet outlets, are fine for adding some depth of flavor to a vinaigrette or sauce. One of my favorite tricks is to pour a whole bottle of the stuff into a saucepan and reduce it by at least half. This will concentrate the flavor and give it a syrupy consistency that's great with roasted meats or over poached pears or strawberries. If I happen to have a leftover vanilla bean lying around, I'll stick that in the jar with the reduced balsamic. It just adds a little secret something.

I love to put a dab of mustard in a vinaigrette because it adds flavor and helps keep the dressing from separating into an oil layer and a vinegar layer. That little dollop of spicy mustard will help the salad emulsify temporarily when you give it a vigorous shake or whisk. I'm working through the last of my hoarded jars of the fabulous TJ's Hot and Sweet Mustard, which they've recently discontinued. JOE! You done me wrong here, and I am mounting a campaign to bring this glorious elixir back! In the meantime, I've recommended Dijon mustard in the dressing recipes, but if the beloved Hot and Sweet Mustard returns, by all means, use that.

Whether salad is a side dish or the showpiece of the meal, you'll find great inspiration for ingredients on Joe's shelves. A handful of nuts or dried fruit, a crumble of savory cheese, and a whisk of freshly made vinaigrette, and you've created a masterpiece of healthful goodness.

NECTARINE, GORGONZOLA, and GREENS

 Nectarines are my favorite fruit, and for the brief period that they're perfect, I could eat them at every meal. Here's a way to sneak them onto the lunch or dinner table, where their golden glow will perk up your spirits.

1 (7-ounce) bag arugula

2 ripe nectarines (or peaches), cut into wedges

¼ red onion, thinly sliced

¼ cup crumbled Gorgonzola

¼ cup toasted walnuts

1 tablespoon red wine vinegar

2 teaspoons Dijon mustard

3 tablespoons olive oil

salt and freshly ground black pepper

VEGETARIAN

Arrange the arugula on a platter. Place the nectarine wedges around the platter. Scatter the sliced red onion, crumbled Gorgonzola, and walnuts over the salad. Whisk together the vinegar and mustard, then, whisking continuously, add the olive oil in a thin stream. Taste the dressing on a leaf of arugula and adjust seasoning with salt and pepper. Lightly dress the salad and serve.

Serves: 4

Prep Time: 10 minutes

Cooking Time: none

Try adding grilled steak strips, cooked chicken, or roast pork to this.

SWEET POTATO, PECAN, and CRANBERRY SALAD

The vibrant, earthy orange of the sweet potatoes paired with the deep red of the cranberries is so pretty that this is a dish you'll definitely eat with your eyes. Full of antioxidants, this salad is both gorgeous and good for you.

1 sweet potato, cubed

drizzle of olive oil

1 tablespoon Dijon mustard

1 teaspoon honey

2 tablespoons red wine vinegar

⅓ cup olive oil

1 (5-ounce) bag Herb Salad Mix
or Baby Spring Mix salad greens

½ cup candied pecans

handful of dried cranberries
or cherries

handful of crumbled feta
or blue cheese

salt and pepper

VEGETARIAN

Preheat oven to 425°F. Toss sweet potato cubes with olive oil, salt, and pepper. Place in a single layer on a baking sheet and roast until tender, about 20 minutes. (Or use leftover roasted sweet potatoes for this purpose.) In a small bowl, whisk together the mustard, honey, and vinegar. Stream in oil, whisking constantly. Toss greens with a little dressing and arrange on a platter. Scatter candied pecans and cranberries or cherries over the greens and top with roasted sweet potatoes. Drizzle with a little more dressing and garnish with crumbled cheese.

Serves: 4
Prep Time: 10 minutes
Cooking Time: 20 minutes

CRAYON-BOX TOMATO and CANDIED NUT SALAD

The name comes from the fabulous, vibrant colors of the cherry tomatoes. I was never a fan of these little spurt-and-seed bombs until TJ's cherry tomatoes lured me in. These babies are packed with flavor and just enough acidity to perk things up.

handful of haricots verts (French green beans) or regular green beans

1 (16-ounce) container Trader Joe's Mixed Medley Cherry Tomatoes (multicolored)

½ cup chopped Italian parsley

½ cup candied walnuts or pecans, coarsely chopped

1 tablespoon red wine vinegar

¼ cup olive oil

⅓ cup crumbled feta or goat cheese

pomegranate arils, for garnish (optional)

VEGETARIAN

Steam the green beans in a steamer over boiling water until tender. This will take 6 to 8 minutes for haricots verts and a few minutes longer for regular green beans. Rinse under cold water to stop the cooking process and set the color. Cut medium-sized and larger cherry tomatoes in half and place in a bowl or platter with the cooked beans. Add the parsley and candied nuts. Toss to combine. Whisk together the vinegar and oil and drizzle over tomato mixture. Crumble the cheese over the top and garnish with pomegranate arils, if using.

Serves: 4
Prep Time: less than 10 minutes
Cooking Time: none

This is a great side salad, but try it as a relish with grilled fish or steak, too.

WINTER HOLIDAY SALAD

Mâche (pronounced "mosh," like a mosh pit) is one of my favorite greens, and in my area, TJ's is the only place to get it. It looks like a cluster of petals, and the nutty flavor and soft texture are wonderful in winter salads.

1 tablespoon Trader Joe's Orange Muscat Champagne Vinegar

2 teaspoons Dijon mustard

3 tablespoons olive oil

1 (4-ounce) bag mâche (or other tender greens)

1 ruby grapefruit, segmented

½ ripe avocado, sliced

2 ounces goat cheese, sliced in ½-inch-thick rounds

handful of pomegranate arils

handful of candied pecans or Tsao Nuts (page 15)

salt and pepper

VEGETARIAN

Whisk together the vinegar and mustard and drizzle in olive oil, whisking constantly. Season with salt and pepper. Toss mâche with a little of the dressing and arrange on plates or a platter. Scatter the grapefruit segments and avocado slices on top and drizzle with a little more dressing. Place rounds of goat cheese on top of salad, scatter pomegranate arils and candied pecans on top, and drizzle with a little more dressing.

Serves: 4

Prep Time: less than 10 minutes

Cooking Time: none

••

For a fancier presentation, press the pomegranate arils (great Scrabble word!) into the sides of the goat cheese log before you cut the rounds. It will look jewel encrusted.

••

ALL-ABOUT-TJ'S SALAD

This is one of those "add and subtract" salads. Don't like beets? You can leave 'em out. (But please, won't you try them? They taste nothing like the ones from a can!) If you prefer blue cheese, skip the goat cheese and scatter crumbled Gorgonzola or Maytag blue on top. Got some leftover roast chicken? Great—toss that in, too!

½ cup pepitas
(roasted pumpkin seeds)

1 (5-ounce) log goat cheese
(Trader Joe's Chèvre, Madame
Chèvre, or Silver Goat Chèvre)

½ (4-ounce) bag mâche

½ (7-ounce) bag arugula

1 (8-ounce) box Trader Joe's
precooked Baby Beets, cubed (in
the salad and vegetable section)

handful of dried cherries

DRESSING

2 teaspoons Dijon mustard

drizzle of honey (optional)

2 tablespoons Orange Muscat
Champagne Vinegar

⅓ cup canola or grapeseed oil

salt and pepper

VEGETARIAN, GLUTEN-FREE

Chop the pepitas coarsely (with a knife or in a food processor). Put the chopped seeds on a cutting board or parchment sheet and roll the log of goat cheese in the seeds to coat thoroughly. Set aside. In a small bowl, whisk together the mustard (and honey if using) and vinegar. Drizzle in the oil, whisking constantly. Adjust seasoning to taste with salt and pepper. Dress the greens very lightly and arrange on salad plates. Dress the beets with a little more of the dressing and scatter over greens. Cut the seed-coated goat cheese into ½-inch-thick rounds and place a slice atop each salad. Scatter dried cherries on top.

Serves: 4
Prep Time: less than 10 minutes
Cooking Time: none

Dental floss works great for cutting the goat cheese—just make sure to use the plain version, not the minty-fresh!

AVOCADO, ORANGE, and OLIVE SALAD

The creaminess of avocado pairs so well with the tang of citrus, and the olives bring salt and a counterpoint of color. This is a great addition to a tapas-party menu.

2 ripe avocados, sliced lengthwise

2 oranges, peeled, and sliced into wheels

1 cup pitted black or green olives

DRESSING:

juice of 2 limes

2 tablespoons olive oil

pinch of ground cumin

VEGETARIAN, VEGAN, GLUTEN-FREE

Arrange avocado slices and orange wheels on a plate. Scatter the olives over the top. Whisk together the lime juice, olive oil, and cumin. Drizzle over salad.

Serves: 4
Prep Time: less than 10 minutes
Cooking Time: none

If you make this in winter, when blood oranges are in season, the colors will make you swoon with pleasure.

GREEN BEAN, TOMATO, and OLIVE SALAD

Even when regular tomatoes are looking anemic, the multicolored cherry tomatoes at Trader Joe's are vibrant and tasty. This salad is good served warm, at room temperature, or cold the next day.

1 pound green beans, trimmed

½ cup olive oil

2 tablespoons red wine vinegar

8 ounces Trader Joe's Mixed Medley Cherry Tomatoes (multicolored)

½ cup olives (green, black, or both, pitted or not)

¼ cup feta cheese, crumbled

salt and pepper

VEGETARIAN, GLUTEN-FREE

Steam the green beans in a steamer over boiling water until just tender, about 8 to 10 minutes. Place in a bowl and toss with olive oil, then with the vinegar. Add the tomatoes, olives, and feta, and toss again. Season to taste with salt and pepper. (The feta and olives are salty, so season accordingly.)

Serves: 4
Prep Time: 10 minutes
Cooking Time: 10 minutes

WARM MUSHROOM SALAD

A study in autumn tones, the creamy, warm mushrooms create an amazingly lush dressing for the greens. This salad is among the most popular recipes we've ever presented at Chez Cherie. Students tell me they use it all the time for entertaining. Nothing could make me happier!

2 ounces bacon or pancetta

1 shallot, thinly sliced

8 ounces fresh mushrooms, cleaned and sliced (I like a mix of crimini, shiitake, and portabella.)

2 tablespoons red wine vinegar

½ (7.5-ounce) container crème fraîche

1 (5-ounce) bag mixed baby greens, such as Baby Spring Mix or Herb Salad Mix

handful of shredded carrots

salt and pepper

GLUTEN-FREE

Chop the bacon or pancetta and sauté over medium-high heat in a medium sauté pan until beginning to crisp, about 3 minutes. Add the shallot and sauté another minute, until fragrant. Add the sliced mushrooms and reduce heat to medium. Continue to sauté 5 to 6 minutes. (At first, the mushrooms will absorb the bacon drippings and will appear dry. After a few minutes, they will release some of their juices and will appear moister. At this point, they will begin to soften and cook.) Season the mushrooms with salt and pepper as they cook. When the mushrooms are tender, add the vinegar and cook 2 minutes. Add the crème fraîche and warm through. Adjust seasonings to taste. Arrange the greens on a platter and scatter shredded carrots over them. Top with the warm mushrooms. They'll wilt the greens slightly, and the sauce will dress the greens.

Serves: 4
Prep Time: 15 minutes
Cooking Time: less than 15 minutes

....

A slice of bacon is about an ounce, so two will do nicely for this recipe. You might want to cook an extra for the cook's treat!

....

ASIAN FLAVORS SLAW

This slaw is great on its own, but I especially love it with some leftover roasted pork tenderloin or roasted chicken on top. Shrimp works, too!

3 cups shredded green cabbage

1 cup shredded carrots

1 red bell pepper, cut into thin strips

2 green onions, shredded

¼ cup cilantro, coarsely chopped

1 tablespoon grapeseed or canola oil

1 tablespoon toasted sesame oil

2 tablespoons soy sauce

1 tablespoon rice vinegar

2 teaspoons brown sugar

1 jalapeño, minced

2 cubes frozen crushed garlic

1 teaspoon Trader Joe's Crushed Ginger (in a jar) or minced ginger

VEGETARIAN, GLUTEN-FREE

In a large bowl, toss together the shredded cabbage, carrots, red bell pepper, green onions, and cilantro. Whisk together the two oils, soy sauce, rice vinegar, brown sugar, minced jalapeño, garlic, and ginger. Toss the salad with the dressing and arrange on a platter.

Serves: 4 to 6
Prep Time: 10 minutes
Cooking Time: none

CARNE ASADA SALAD

This is a one-dish meal salad full of spice and crunch. It's pretty enough to serve when guests are expected but quick enough to throw together before soccer practice.

1 (5-ounce) bag Trader Joe's Herb Salad Mix

1 tablespoon olive oil

1 pound Trader Joe's Carne Asada Autentica, thinly sliced

2 tablespoons red wine vinegar

½ (13.75-ounce) jar Trader Joe's Corn and Chile Tomato-Less Salsa

1 avocado, sliced

½ red onion

handful of Trader Joe's Mixed Medley Cherry Tomatoes (multicolored)

¼ English cucumber, thinly sliced

salt and pepper

Arrange lettuce on a platter. Heat the olive oil in a large sauté pan and sauté the meat over medium-high heat until rare. Remove the meat from the pan and arrange over the greens. Add the vinegar to the pan and heat through. Tumble the corn salsa, avocado, red onion, tomatoes, and cucumber on top of the meat and season to taste with salt and pepper. Drizzle the hot vinegar over the salad.

Serves: 4
Prep Time: 10 minutes
Cooking Time: less than 10 minutes

SAUSAGE SALAD *for a* HOT SUMMER NIGHT

Chris is one of my kitchen goddesses at the cooking school. She is my "swan," who always appears to be gliding serenely even though she may be paddling like crazy underneath. The dressing, which is her creation, is her house dressing. It's zingy and lower in fat than most dressings, since the maple syrup decreases the amount of oil used in traditional vinaigrettes.

CHRIS'S TRADER JOE'S SALAD DRESSING:

1 to 2 shallots (use 2 if they are tiny)

¼ cup Trader Joe's Orange Muscat Champagne Vinegar

¼ cup maple syrup or Trader Joe's Maple Agave Syrup Blend

1 tablespoon Dijon mustard

½ cup olive oil

FOR THE SALAD:

½ (8-ounce) package fresh haricots verts (French green beans)

1 teaspoon olive oil

½ pound precooked sausages (Smoked Apple Chardonnay Chicken, Sweet Bell Pepper and Onion Chicken Sausage, or any type you like), sliced into ½-inch rounds

3 to 4 ripe apricots or plums, quartered

1 (5-ounce) bag Trader Joe's Herb Salad Mix (or other soft-leaf lettuce mix)

shaved Parmesan cheese, for garnish (optional)

GLUTEN-FREE

CHRIS'S TRADER JOE'S SALAD DRESSING: In food processor, with motor running, drop in the shallots, then add the rest of the ingredients and process until blended.

FOR THE SALAD: Steam the green beans in a steamer over boiling water until barely tender, about 6 to 8 minutes. Drain and rinse under cold water to stop the cooking process and set the color. Set aside. In a medium sauté pan, heat the olive oil and sauté the sausages over medium-high heat until warmed and slightly browned, about 5 minutes. Add the fruit and sauté 2 to 3 minutes, until warmed and slightly browned. Place the greens in a bowl and dress lightly with some of the dressing. Arrange on a platter or individual plates. Drizzle a little more dressing over the sausage, fruit, and green beans, and toss to combine. Scatter the sausage, fruit, and green beans over the salad and garnish with shaved Parmesan, if desired.

Serves: 4
Prep Time: 15 minutes
Cooking Time: less than 15 minutes

••

Give that bottle of vinegar a good shake before using, because there's a lot of good flavor settling at the bottom. This dressing will keep in the refrigerator for several days, and it's good as a salad dressing or as a marinade for chicken or pork.

••

SAUSAGE *and* SPUDS SALAD

Another meat-and-potatoes salad that is great for tailgating or game-watching. While I lack the sports gene, I'll root for any team that's serving this on the sidelines!

1 pound fingerling, red, or Teeny Tiny potatoes

2 tablespoons olive oil

2 cubes frozen crushed garlic

1 red onion, cut into slivers

1 (12.8-ounce) package cooked Sun-Dried Tomato Chicken Sausage, Smoked Andouille Chicken Sausage, or another precooked sausage you like, cut into 1-inch pieces

3 tablespoons red wine vinegar

1 tablespoon Dijon mustard

⅓ cup olive oil

1 bag baby spinach (or other salad greens)

GLUTEN-FREE

Preheat oven to 425°F. Cut the potatoes into quarters if they are large or in half if they are small. Toss the potatoes with the olive oil, garlic, and red onion. Arrange in a single layer on a rimmed baking sheet and roast until the potatoes are nearly tender, about 15 minutes. Add the sausage pieces and roast another 10 minutes, until sausage is warmed through and starting to brown. While the vegetables (and sausage) cook, whisk together the red wine vinegar and mustard. Drizzle in the olive oil, whisking constantly. When the vegetables and sausage are cooked, toss them with all but two tablespoons of the vinaigrette. Toss the spinach (or salad greens) with the remaining vinaigrette. Arrange the leaves on a platter or individual plates and top with the roasted vegetables and sausages.

Serves: 4
Prep Time: 10 minutes
Cooking Time: 25 minutes

PUMPKIN *and* CARNITAS SALAD

I like to make this as soon as there is a nip in the air. It looks and tastes like October! If you ask me, we don't eat nearly enough pumpkin. Break out of the pumpkin pie rut and discover the joys of roasted pumpkin. It has become one of my favorite fall vegetables.

1 small pie pumpkin

1 red onion, thinly sliced

about 5 tablespoons olive oil, divided

½ (7-ounce) bag arugula

½ (10-ounce) bag red or green cabbage

1 tablespoon red wine vinegar

¾ (12-ounce) package Trader Jose's Traditional Carnitas

Asiago or Parmesan cheese, for garnish

salt and pepper

Preheat oven (convection, if available) to 425°F. Wash the pumpkin and cut off the four "cheeks," so that all you have is the pumpkin meat, leaving the seeds and strings behind. Cut the quarters into 1-inch crescents and remove the skin, if desired. Toss the pumpkin pieces and red onion slices in about 2 tablespoons of olive oil, and season with salt and pepper. Place on a baking sheet and roast until soft and beginning to caramelize, about 18 minutes. Remove and set aside. Combine the arugula and cabbage in a bowl and toss with the red wine vinegar and remaining olive oil. Arrange greens on a platter or individual plates. Top with roasted pumpkin and red onion. Microwave the carnitas for 3 minutes or sauté over medium-high heat for 5 minutes, until it reaches desired doneness. Shred or chop and scatter over the salad. Shave Asiago or Parmesan cheese over the salad and serve.

Serves: 4
Prep Time: 15 minutes
Cooking Time: less than 20 minutes

You won't use all of the carnitas for this salad, so there'll be leftovers for a taco or two. The salad is delicious without the carnitas, too—but you'll have to change the name of the recipe!

GRILLED FLATBREAD SALAD

The flatbread forms an edible plate to hold the crisp greens and the tangy dressing. The vinaigrette flavors the pizza-style crust, making a crunchy treat. The fun presentation makes this salad a winner at any table. Look for the pizza dough with the prepared salads and sandwiches, not in the frozen foods section.

1 pound Trader Joe's Pizza Dough (Plain, Whole Wheat, or Herb and Garlic)

1 tablespoon red wine vinegar

1 teaspoon Dijon mustard

3 tablespoons olive oil

1 (5-ounce) bag salad greens, such as Baby Spring Mix or Herb Salad Mix

1 ripe avocado, sliced

¼ English cucumber, sliced

½ red onion, sliced

handful of Trader Joe's Mixed Medley Cherry Tomatoes (multicolored)

VEGETARIAN
(if no meat is added)

Preheat a grill to high heat and brush grates with a brass-bristled brush to clean well. Form the pizza dough into 4 to 6 rustic rectangles. When the grill is hot, place the dough on the grill and cook until grill marks are visible and the dough is set on the bottom, about 3 minutes. Flip the dough over and cook on the second side until crisp, another 2 to 3 minutes. Set aside.

Whisk together the red wine vinegar and mustard. Drizzle in the olive oil, whisking as you do so. Toss the salad greens with a little bit of the dressing and arrange on top of the grilled flatbread. Arrange the remaining ingredients on top of the greens and drizzle with more dressing.

Serves: 4
Prep Time: 10 minutes
Cooking Time: less than 10 minutes

• •

If protein is desired, add ¼ to ½ pound sliced grilled flank steak, tri-tip, or pork tenderloin, cooked shrimp, or Trader Joe's Just Chicken.

• •

ARUGULA, CHICKEN, and WALNUT SALAD

Most chicken salads are mayo-intensive, but this one is light on its feet, with a hot vinaigrette to perk it up. This is great for lunch with friends or a summer supper when it's too hot to heat up the oven.

½ (7-ounce) bag arugula

⅓ cup olive oil, divided

1 pound boneless, skinless chicken (breast or thigh), cut into bite-sized pieces

1 cup red bell pepper strips

3 tablespoons red wine vinegar

½ cup walnut pieces

2 teaspoons rosemary, chopped

Parmesan cheese, for garnish

GLUTEN-FREE

Arrange arugula on a serving platter. Heat 2 tablespoons of the olive oil in a large sauté pan and sauté the chicken pieces over medium-high heat until nearly cooked through, about 5 minutes. Add the red bell pepper strips and sauté an additional 2 to 3 minutes, until tender. Add the vinegar and sauté until bits of food stuck to the bottom of the pan release. Pour the pan contents over the arugula. In the same pan, heat the remaining olive oil and add the walnuts and rosemary. Sauté until fragrant, about 3 minutes, and pour over the chicken. Shave Parmesan cheese on top, as desired.

Serves: 4
Prep Time: 15 minutes
Cooking Time: less than 10 minutes

SOUP

"**B**eautiful, beautiful soup" sang Lewis Carroll's Mock Turtle, and I echo his ode to this simple, satisfying meal in a bowl. At Trader Joe's, there are premade soups in the salad and sandwich refrigerated case, and there are soups in the frozen case. There are soups in round-bellied cans and soups in shelf-stable Tetra packs. There are soups that are satisfying on their own and soups that beg to be gussied up.

My favorite items on the soup front are the premade broths, from which a quick soup can be made in moments. The rectangular containers of chicken, vegetable, and beef broth are ready to go. There are 4 cups of broth in each package, and the sodium content is reasonable, compared to canned broth (or stock) or bouillon cubes.

But my very hottest "stock tip" is the relatively new Savory Broth concentrates. Available in beef, chicken, and vegetable flavors, these little foil tubes are packaged in a small box labeled "Reduced Sodium Liquid Concentrate." While that may not sing a culinary song to your ears, these are a boon to the home cook who just doesn't have the time or inclination to simmer bones and vegetables to make broth from scratch. There are a dozen small tubes in a box, which makes them more economical than the larger containers. The contents of each tube can be reconstituted with a cup of water, so one package makes 12 cups of broth. What I like most about this product is its versatility. If you want a stronger chicken flavor, use ¾ cup of water. For a quick, flavorful pan sauce, use a little wine along with a little water, and the results will be deep and rich. (It ain't demi-glace, but it's a good, accessible weeknight substitute for a home cook without access to a restaurant pantry.)

You can also use Savory Broth concentrates to start a real, homemade stock on the occasions when you've got time, inclination, and a stash of bones and vegetables all assembled. Fill a big stockpot with the bones and a few carrots, celery stalks, and an onion, cover with cold water and bring to a simmer. With a few squeezes of broth concentrate, you are on your way to a fragrant pot of soup magic. Of course, you can freeze this homemade culinary gold in small containers to use whenever you want to serve forth an especially wonderful pot of something simmered.

I advise using your TJ's hoarding skills to stockpile a number of these handy boxes of soup starter, because we never know when they might disappear from the shelves.

PERLINE PASTA, PROSCIUTTO, *and* PEA SOUP

 This tasty bowlful of goodness is light, yet full of flavor. The look of this soup just makes me smile—I love how the little pasta purses bob in the broth.

4 cups chicken broth

½ (10-ounce) container Trader Joe's Perline Pasta and Prosciutto

handful of frozen peas

2 handfuls of shredded carrots

red chile pepper flakes

salt and pepper

In a medium saucepan, bring the broth to a boil. Add the perline pasta and the peas, and simmer 3 to 4 minutes until the pasta is nearly cooked (taste one to make sure). Add the carrots and simmer until tender, 1 to 2 minutes. Season to taste with salt, pepper, and red chile pepper flakes.

If you happen to have a Parmesan rind lurking in your cheese drawer, toss that in to simmer with the soup. It deepens the flavor of the broth.

CREAMY TOMATO and ROASTED RED PEPPER SOUP with PESTO GNOCCHI

This soup can be made in the time it takes to read the recipe through once. The pillowy gnocchi are soft in the mouth, and the pesto adds great color and flavor. Plus, it's so pretty and satisfying, you'll make it over and over.

1 (32-ounce) container Trader Joe's Tomato and Roasted Red Pepper Soup

4 ounces mascarpone

⅓ (6.17-ounce) package potato gnocchi

about 4 tablespoons Trader Giotto's Pesto alla Genovese (in the refrigerated case)

salt and pepper

VEGETARIAN

Heat the soup, then stir in the mascarpone. While the soup heats, bring a small pot of water to a boil. Add the gnocchi and boil just until they bob to the surface, 3 to 4 minutes. Scoop them out and set aside. Season the soup to taste with salt and pepper, ladle into bowls, and add a few gnocchi to each serving. Drizzle a little pesto into each serving.

Serves: 4
Prep Time: 5 minutes
Cooking Time: 10 minutes

PAPPA AL POMODORO RICCO

One November, we took a dream trip to Tuscany with a group of students. We picked olives, we hunted for truffles in the woods, we ate amazing food. Pappa al pomodoro was a frequent offering—each version was different and delicious. No exact measurements on this one—engage your "inner Tuscan" and make it by eye!

olive oil

3 cubes frozen crushed garlic

3 (14-ounce) cans chopped tomatoes

water or chicken broth

sage or basil leaves (optional)

2 large handfuls stale bread (2½ to 3 cups ciabatta or another artisanal bread)

VEGETARIAN AND VEGAN
(if made with water)

In a wide, shallow pan, heat about 2 tablespoons of olive oil and sauté the garlic over medium-high heat until fragrant. Add the tomatoes along with a canful of water or chicken broth (use one of the tomato cans). Break up the tomatoes with a wooden spoon. (If using sage—recommended for fall or winter—add some whole sprigs, tied together with kitchen twine.) Bring to a boil, reduce heat, and simmer 15 minutes. Tear the stale bread into small pieces and add to the pan. Stir well and simmer 10 minutes. Add more water or broth as needed, but the consistency should be thick—almost like oatmeal. Season with salt and pepper, and stir in about ¼ cup olive oil. (Remove sage, if used.) Ladle into serving bowls and drizzle with more olive oil. Scatter with torn basil leaves, if desired, in spring and summer.

Serves: 4 to 6
Prep Time: 5 minutes
Cooking Time: less than 30 minutes

THANKSGIVING *in a* BOWL

Some TJ's ingredients are seasonal, but many are shelf-stable, so you can stockpile the ones you love. The fried onion pieces will crunch up casseroles, salads, and even sandwiches, so grab a few before they disappear with the holidays!

1 (32-ounce) container Trader Joe's Butternut Apple Soup (or Sweet Potato Bisque or Butternut Squash Soup)

1 (7.5-ounce) container crème fraîche

2 tablespoons bourbon

2 ounces smoked turkey breast, cut into slivers

about ¼ cup Trader Joe's Gourmet Fried Onion Pieces

salt and pepper

In a medium saucepan, warm the soup with the crème fraîche and bourbon. Season to taste with salt and pepper, and garnish with slivers of turkey and a few fried onion pieces.

Serves: 4
Prep Time: 5 minutes
Cooking Time: 10 minutes

POTSTICKER SOUP

When I feel a cold coming on, I set a pot of this soup on the stove to simmer. It may not be a cure, but at least psychologically it does the trick. The steam seems to clear my head, and the warming broth is satisfying and makes me feel comforted, as soup always does.

4 cups chicken or vegetable broth

1 tablespoon rice vinegar

1 tablespoon soy sauce

2 cubes frozen crushed garlic

½ (16-ounce) package frozen chicken or vegetable potstickers (about 12)

1 (20-ounce) bag stir-fry vegetables

½ cup shredded carrots

4 green onions, thinly sliced

2 teaspoons sesame oil

VEGETARIAN *(if vegetable broth and vegetarian potstickers are used)*

In a medium saucepan, combine broth, rice vinegar, soy sauce, and garlic. Bring to a boil. Add potstickers and bring back to a boil. Reduce heat and simmer 4 minutes. Add stir-fry vegetables and carrots and simmer until vegetables are tender and potstickers are cooked through, about 3 minutes. Garnish with green onions and a drizzle of sesame oil.

Serves: 4 to 6
Prep Time: 5 minutes
Cooking Time: 15 minutes

ALMOST-FROM-SCRATCH BUTTERNUT SQUASH SOUP *with* BOURBON

This squash soup tastes like it was an all-day project but comes together in a snap, especially if you use the packages of precut squash in the produce section. Be sure to get really fresh ones (check the expiration date), as squash keeps a long while in its whole state, but once it's cut, it becomes quite perishable. Buy it only one or two days before you use it, at most.

1 tablespoon olive oil

1 large red onion, chopped

2 pounds butternut or acorn squash, peeled and cut into 1-inch cubes

1 russet potato, peeled and cut into 1-inch cubes

4 cups chicken or vegetable broth

2 tablespoons bourbon

2 tablespoons heavy cream (optional)

pinch of red chile pepper flakes

salt and white pepper

VEGETARIAN *(if made with vegetable broth)*, VEGAN *(if made with vegetable broth and no cream)*, GLUTEN-FREE

Heat the olive oil in a stockpot, and sauté the red onion over medium-high heat, about 5 minutes. Add the squash, potato, and broth, and bring to a boil. Add a pinch of salt, reduce heat to low, cover, and simmer until vegetables are soft, about 20 minutes. Purée, preferably using an immersion blender. (To purée in a food processor, strain, reserving liquid and solids, and purée solids carefully, adding reserved liquid as necessary. Return to stockpot and add remaining liquid until desired consistency is achieved.) Add bourbon and cream (if using), and adjust seasoning to taste with salt, white pepper, and red chile pepper flakes.

Serves: 6 to 8
Prep Time: 10 minutes
Cooking Time: less than 30 minutes

Whole squashes are carried seasonally at TJ's, but you can get the precut cubes in the fresh vegetable section nearly year-round.

HEARTY SHERRIED MUSHROOM SOUP

This soup is rich and creamy, but without a ton of cream. Using both fresh and dried mushrooms brings a silken texture and a deep, smoky flavor to the bowl.

4 tablespoons butter, divided

2 shallots, finely chopped

1 pound fresh mushrooms (crimini, button, shiitake, portabella, or a combination), finely chopped

2 tablespoons flour

1 tablespoon dried mushroom powder made from ½ (.88-ounce) package Trader Joe's Mixed Wild Mushroom Medley (see note)

4 cups vegetable broth

3 tablespoons dry sherry

salt and pepper

crème fraîche, for garnish

VEGETARIAN

In a medium saucepan, melt 2 tablespoons of butter and sauté the shallots over medium-high heat until fragrant, 3 to 4 minutes. Add the chopped mushrooms and sauté until the mushrooms release their liquid and appear a bit dry, about 5 minutes. Remove to a bowl and set aside. In the same saucepan, melt the remaining butter. Add the flour and stir into a paste. Cook over medium-low heat until the flour loses its bleachy aroma, about 3 minutes. Add the dried mushroom powder. Stir to incorporate and cook another minute. Add the sautéed mushrooms and broth, and bring to a boil. Reduce heat, salt and pepper lightly, and simmer 20 minutes. Add the sherry and adjust seasonings to taste. Swirl in a little crème fraîche for garnish.

Serves: 4 to 6
Prep Time: 5 to 10 minutes
Cooking Time: 30 minutes

• •
To make the mushroom powder, grind the dried mushrooms in a coffee grinder until powdered. These are also great for coating fish filets before roasting or sautéing. The intense, smoky taste adds great flavor.
• •

CREAM of CHICKEN SOUP with WILD RICE

A meal in a bowl, this soup is a rib-sticker. Chunky with vegetables and tender chicken, it almost demands a fork.

4 tablespoons butter

2 yellow onions, chopped

1 leek, chopped

2 medium carrots, chopped (or 1 cup shredded carrots)

5 cups chicken broth

¼ cup raw white rice

¼ cup raw wild rice

1 pound raw chicken meat, diced

1 cup heavy cream

1 cup frozen green beans

GLUTEN-FREE

Melt butter in a stockpot. Add onions, leek, and carrots, and cook over low heat, covered, until vegetables are tender, about 10 minutes. Add broth and rice. Bring to a boil, reduce heat, and cover. Simmer 15 minutes, then add the chicken. Simmer 20 to 30 minutes more, until the chicken and rice are cooked through. Add cream and green beans, season with salt and pepper, and simmer another 5 minutes, until green beans are warmed.

Serves: 6 to 8

Prep Time: 10 minutes

Cooking Time: less than an hour

If you substitute the precooked wild rice, this soup can be done in about half the time. Use ¾ to 1 cup of the precooked wild rice and add it when you add the chicken. As soon as the chicken is cooked through (this will depend on how large the pieces are), soup's on!

POTATO-KALE MINESTRA

The sausages are precooked, but sautéing them in the oil adds irresistible color and transmits some of their flavor to the oil, which then carries it throughout the soup. On a cold day, a steaming bowl of this is heaven.

1 tablespoon olive oil

½ pound Trader Joe's Smoked Andouille Chicken Sausage, cut into ½-inch slices

1 onion, diced

2 cubes frozen crushed garlic

1 tablespoon fresh rosemary, minced

1 pound russet potatoes, cubed

rind of Parmesan cheese (optional)

4 cups chicken or vegetable broth

2 cups Trader Joe's Southern Greens Blend or Chard of Many Colors, chopped

salt and pepper

grated Parmesan cheese, for garnish

GLUTEN-FREE

Heat the olive oil in a medium saucepan and sauté the sausages over medium-high heat until browned, about 4 minutes. Set the sausages aside. In the same pan, sauté the onion until fragrant and softened, 5 to 6 minutes. Add the garlic and sauté until fragrant, about 2 minutes. Add the rosemary, potatoes (and Parmesan rind, if using), and broth. Bring liquid to a boil, reduce heat, and simmer about 10 minutes. Add the sausage and simmer until potatoes are tender, about 10 minutes. Add the Southern Greens Blend or chard and simmer until it is wilted and tender, about 5 more minutes. Season to taste with salt and pepper. (Remove the rind, if used.) Ladle into bowls and pass the grated cheese for garnish.

Serves: 4 to 6
Prep Time: 10 minutes
Cooking Time: less than an hour

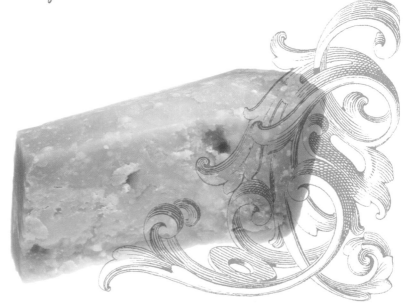

CHILE and CRAB CHOWDER

Rich and satisfying, with some heat to wake and shake those taste buds, this soup is a bowlful of creamy, crabby goodness.

2 tablespoons butter

1 medium onion, chopped

4 cups vegetable or chicken broth

1 medium boiling potato, cubed

1 teaspoon chopped fresh thyme

1 (4-ounce) can Trader Joe's Hatch Valley Fire-Roasted Diced Green Chiles

1 cup corn kernels, fresh or frozen

½ pound Jack's Premium Catch refrigerated canned crabmeat

½ cup half-and-half or heavy cream

½ cup grated sharp cheddar cheese

dash of Trader Joe's Chili Pepper Hot Sauce or Jalapeño Pepper Hot Sauce

salt and pepper

GLUTEN-FREE

Heat the butter in the saucepan over medium-high heat, and sauté the chopped onion until it begins to soften, about 5 minutes. Add the broth, potato, and thyme, and bring to a boil. Reduce heat to low and simmer until potato is tender, about 15 minutes. Stir in the chiles and corn. Add the crabmeat and the half-and-half or cream and warm through. Remove from heat, stir in grated cheddar cheese, and allow the heat of the chowder to melt the cheese. Season to taste with hot sauce, salt, and pepper.

Serves: 4 to 6

Prep Time: 5 minutes

Cooking Time: less than 30 minutes

A boiling potato (labeled Baby Red Potatoes, Baby Dutch Yellow Potatoes, or Potato Medley-Red, Gold, and Purple) has a thinner, smoother skin than a russet, or baking, potato. These babies will hold their shape better when simmered than a russet, which will tend to fall apart.

KEVIN'S FAVORITE PUMPKIN BLACK BEAN SOUP

This recipe originated from a recipe published in a cooking magazine about 20 years ago. (I wish I could remember which one, so I could give it due credit!) It was in the "to try" pile for several years, and I finally got around to making it at the end of soup season. It was a big hit, especially with my son Kevin, who was in third grade then. But soup season is short in Southern California, so we didn't have another pot for months and months. Finally, I got a chance to stir up another batch, and as soon as he burst through the door after school, he slung his backpack down, sniffed the air, and asked, "Is that the really good soup I liked?" Those olfactory memories linger on in our brains, and this one is sure to create fond food memories!

3 (15-ounce) cans black beans, drained

1 (15-ounce) can tomatoes, chopped

4 tablespoons butter

2 small onions, finely chopped

3 shallots, chopped

1 tablespoon ground cumin

4 cubes frozen crushed garlic

4 cups beef broth

1 (12-ounce) can pumpkin

½ cup dry sherry

½ pound cooked ham or smoked turkey, cubed

splash of balsamic vinegar

crème fraîche and toasted pumpkin seeds, for garnish

salt and pepper

GLUTEN-FREE

In a food processor, coarsely chop the black beans and tomatoes. Set aside.

In a stockpot, melt the butter and sauté the onion, shallots, and cumin over medium heat until the onion is soft and beginning to brown, about 8 to 10 minutes. Add the garlic and sauté just until fragrant, 1 to 2 minutes. Stir in the bean-tomato mixture. Season lightly with salt and pepper. Add the broth, pumpkin, and sherry. Simmer, uncovered, 25 minutes or until thick enough to coat a spoon. Just before serving, add ham or turkey and vinegar and season to taste with salt and pepper. Garnish with a swirl of crème fraîche and a sprinkle of pumpkin seeds.

Serves: 6 to 8

Prep Time: 10 minutes

Cooking Time: less than an hour

Chapter 4

BEANS, RICE, GRAINS, AND POTATOES

The grains section of Trader Joe's has a different selection of products almost every time I visit, so it's a fun place to experiment with new meal ideas. From plain white rice to several special mixtures, like the Harvest Grains Blend, the bags promise tasty meals or sides in the making. The ancient and very healthful quinoa is there to test your pronunciation skills—it's "keen-wha"—and it's practically a miracle food. Although it is treated as a grain, it's really a seed from a leafy plant similar to spinach, and it's a complete protein, so it's great for people limiting or eliminating meat from their diets. Quinoa's creamy, slightly nutty texture makes it super for salads and for serving alongside roasted or grilled meats. It's terrific for breakfast (think oatmeal) with some agave syrup drizzled over it or with a dollop of one of Trader Joe's excellent yogurts.

If cooking rice is your culinary Waterloo, or if time is just too short, TJ's carries precooked rice in several forms. The vacuum-sealed, shelf-stable wild rice is quite a time-saver, since wild rice can take 45 minutes to an hour to reach the toothsome tender state. One of the biggest sellers is the frozen rice. Now, I first heard about this when I overheard a customer complaining about it being out of stock. My snooty chef-brain (which lays low almost all the time but rears its ugly head on rare occasions) shot imaginary fireworks into the air. "Frozen RICE? Who is lazy enough to need *frozen rice*? That's only one step up from the plastic-wrapped russet potatoes at the grocery store, already prepped for the microwave." Luckily, this was internal monologue, so no one came to blows. Next time I was in the store, I checked it out and saw that not only did they have frozen white rice, they had frozen *brown* rice. Well now, that's an entirely different kettle of fish—or pot of rice! Brown rice, like wild rice, takes a *long* time to cook. Since I was looking to lose a few pounds, and brown rice is not only healthful but tends to fill me up fast, I was curious. Inside the gigantic cardboard box, there were three plastic-clad portions. Poke the obligatory hole, pop in the microwave, and a mere three minutes later, I had nutty, tasty, fluffy brown rice. A scoop of my beloved Corn and Chile Tomato-Less Salsa on top, and I had a zippy, tasty lunch that saw me happily through weeks of that dieting period. I *can* cook brown rice, of course, but it takes 40 minutes or more. Do you know how many Jelly Bellies I can eat in 40 minutes while waiting for that blasted brown rice to be done? Be sure to buy the frozen brown rice when you see it because it is hard to keep in stock.

The selection of grains at Trader Joe's is ever-evolving, and these bags of goodness keep well, so I try to visit that area of the store frequently and stock up on a bag or box of something new or an old favorite. Israeli couscous will keep a long while, and I never know if it will be going-going-gone from the aisle. Hoarding, people … not a pretty word, but it's part of the strategy of shopping at TJ's!

BLACK BEAN SALAD

This is a great make-and-take salad. For Music in the Park, seaside picnics, or just for brown-baggin' it, this salad is perfect because it's tasty cold or at room temperature.

2 (15-ounce) cans black beans, drained and rinsed

3 stalks celery, chopped

1 red onion, chopped

1 (¾-ounce) package fresh cilantro, chopped

1 teaspoon ground cumin

¼ teaspoon red chile pepper flakes, crushed

2 tablespoons Trader Joe's Orange Muscat Champagne Vinegar or red wine vinegar

1 teaspoon Dijon mustard

½ cup olive oil

salt and pepper

VEGETARIAN, VEGAN, GLUTEN-FREE

In a medium bowl, combine the black beans, celery, red onion, and cilantro. In a separate bowl, combine the cumin, crushed red chile pepper flakes, vinegar, and Dijon mustard, then whisk in the olive oil and toss with the bean mixture. Season to taste with salt and pepper.

Serves: 4 to 6
Prep Time: 15 minutes
Cooking Time: none

CORN *and* BASIL RICE

*Summer on a fork. This rice dish is quick, and even quicker
if you use Trader Joe's frozen rice.*

2 cups water or chicken broth

1 cup Trader Joe's Thai Jasmine
Rice or basmati rice (or omit
water or broth and use 3 cups
cooked rice)

1 tablespoon butter

kernels from 1 ear of corn (or ¾
cup frozen roasted corn)

2 tablespoons basil leaves,
chiffonaded

salt and pepper

VEGETARIAN, VEGAN *(if made
with water)*, GLUTEN-FREE

Bring water or broth to a boil in a small saucepan.
Stir in the rice and bring back to a boil. Cover the pan,
reduce the heat to low, and cook, without lifting the lid,
for 15 minutes. Turn off the heat, do not lift the lid, and
let stand 5 to 10 minutes. In a small sauté pan, heat the
butter and sauté the corn over medium-high heat until
warmed through, 2 to 3 minutes for fresh corn or about
5 minutes for frozen corn. Fluff the rice with a fork and
toss in the corn to combine. Season to taste with salt and
pepper and garnish with basil just before serving.

Serves: 2 to 4
Prep Time: 5 minutes
Cooking Time: 20 minutes, if cooking rice from scratch

• •

This makes a great base for a rice salad—just add some
cooked chicken or shrimp and a little vinegar or fresh-squeezed
lemon juice.

• •

WILD RICE *with* SHIITAKES

There's something about combining rice and mushrooms that brings out the best of both. The earthy mushroom flavor brings depth to the fluffy, steamy rice grains. Any leftovers make a great snack the next day.

2 tablespoons butter

2 shallots, chopped

1 (3.5-ounce) package shiitake mushrooms, chopped

⅔ cup raw wild rice

2 teaspoons fresh thyme leaves

2 cups beef broth (or chicken broth or water)

salt and pepper

VEGETARIAN *(if water is used)*, GLUTEN-FREE

In a medium saucepan, melt the butter and sauté shallots and mushrooms over medium-high heat until softened, about 5 minutes. Set vegetables aside. In the same saucepan, add wild rice, thyme leaves, and broth. Bring to a boil. Reduce heat, cover, and simmer about 45 minutes, until rice is tender and liquid is absorbed. (Drain off excess liquid, if necessary.) Stir in sautéed mushrooms and shallots and adjust seasoning to taste with salt and pepper.

In a rush? Grab the precooked wild rice package, sauté the shallots and mushrooms, and sprinkle in the thyme leaves.

QUICK BLACK BEANS *and* RICE

So fast, so full of flavor. This is great as an accompaniment to any Latin-American or Spanish main dish, or simply folded into a warm tortilla. Pass the cheese, please!

1 tablespoon olive oil

2 cubes frozen crushed garlic

pinch dried oregano

pinch ground cumin

1 (15-ounce) can black beans, drained

juice of 1 lime

salt and pepper

3 cups cooked white or brown rice

2 tablespoons chopped cilantro (optional)

VEGETARIAN, VEGAN, GLUTEN-FREE

In a medium sauté pan, heat the oil and sauté the garlic until fragrant, 2 to 3 minutes. Add the oregano and cumin and sauté another minute. Add the drained black beans and sauté to warm through. Remove from heat and squeeze in lime juice. Adjust seasonings to taste with salt and pepper, and mound on top of hot cooked rice. Garnish with cilantro, if desired.

Serves: 4
Prep Time: 5 minutes
Cooking Time: 5 minutes

BRENNA'S NUTTY and WILD RICE SALAD

My daughter, Brenna, can eat her weight's worth of this crunchy, nutty salad.

4 cups chicken broth (or water)

1 cup wild rice, rinsed under cold water (see note)

½ cup chopped green apple (pippin or Granny Smith) or grapes (halved)

1 stalk celery, chopped

¼ red onion, chopped

½ cup toasted hazelnuts, coarsely chopped

½ cup toasted pecans, coarsely chopped

DRESSING:

2 tablespoons red wine vinegar

2 cubes frozen crushed garlic

1 teaspoon Dijon mustard

1 teaspoon honey or agave syrup

½ cup grapeseed or canola oil

¼ cup olive oil

salt and freshly ground black pepper

VEGETARIAN, VEGAN *(if water is used)*, GLUTEN-FREE

Bring the broth (or water) to a boil in a medium saucepan. Add the wild rice and bring back to a boil. Cover, reduce heat to medium-low, and cook until rice is tender, about 45 minutes. In a large bowl, combine chopped apple, celery, red onion, and nuts. Set aside until rice is cooked. When rice is tender, if there is just a little bit of liquid left, let stand until it is absorbed. If there is more than ½ cup, drain the rice into a colander.

FOR DRESSING: In a food processor, combine vinegar, garlic, mustard, and honey or agave syrup. With motor running, drizzle in the oils until emulsified. Add the cooked rice to the chopped apple mixture, then stir in the dressing while the rice is still warm. Adjust seasonings to taste with more vinegar, salt, and black pepper, if necessary.

Serves: 4 to 6

Prep Time: 10 minutes

Cooking Time: 1 hour if cooking wild rice, no cooking time if using precooked rice

If you use precooked wild rice, omit the water or chicken broth and use about 3½ cups of rice.

COUSCOUS *with* DRIED FRUIT

A little Mediterranean in flavor profile, this side dish gets its great texture from the dried fruit mixed with the fluffy couscous. And it's good for ya, too!

2½ cups chicken broth

1 cinnamon stick

¼ cup chopped dried cherries (see note)

¼ cup chopped dried apricots

generous pinch of salt

2 tablespoons butter

1 (17.6-ounce) box Trader Joe's Whole Wheat Couscous

salt and pepper

Place the chicken broth, cinnamon stick, dried fruits, salt, and butter in a medium saucepan, and bring to a boil. Stir in couscous, cover, and remove from heat. Let stand 5 minutes. Fluff with fork. Season to taste with pepper and more salt, if needed.

For a pretty presentation, butter a ramekin and pack the couscous mixture in, then invert onto a dinner plate to serve.

The dried Rainier cherries are seriously addictive—they have an almost caramelly flavor that's extraordinary. They are seasonal, so hoard them when you find them, and use them wherever dried cherries are called for in these recipes. Or just eat them right from the bag. So, so good!

MUSHROOM HAZELNUT RICE

Add-ins are a great way to perk up a bowl of rice. The mushrooms and nuts bring such a satisfying earthiness to this dish, and the lemon zest makes it come alive.

1 tablespoon butter

1 tablespoon olive oil

1 cup fresh or frozen mushrooms, chopped

¼ cup hazelnuts, chopped

2 cubes frozen crushed garlic

4 cups cooked white rice

zest of 1 lemon

salt and pepper

VEGETARIAN, GLUTEN-FREE

Heat the butter and olive oil in a medium sauté pan. Add the mushrooms and sauté over medium heat about 5 minutes. Add the hazelnuts and garlic and sauté until fragrant, 2 to 3 minutes. Add the cooked rice and warm through. Season to taste with salt, pepper, and lemon zest.

Serves: 4 to 6

Prep Time: 5 minutes

Cooking Time: 10 minutes

ISRAELI COUSCOUS

 *I literally yelped with delight when I found Israeli couscous on the shelf at my Joe's. I love this roly-poly, nutty-flavored pasta-grain hybrid. It cooks quickly, looks great on the plate, and is a vehicle for any number of flavor combinations you might dream up. Israeli couscous? Yesyes!*

2 tablespoons butter

½ red onion, chopped

1 (8-ounce) box Trader Joe's Israeli Couscous

2 tubes Trader Joe's chicken or vegetable Savory Broth concentrate

⅓ cup dried cranberries

½ cup pistachios, coarsely chopped

salt and pepper

VEGETARIAN
(if vegetable broth is used)

In a medium sauté pan, melt the butter and sauté the onion over medium-high heat until tender, about 4 minutes. Add the couscous and sauté until golden, another 2 to 3 minutes. Add enough water to cover the couscous and pour in the broth concentrate. Add the dried cranberries and bring to a boil. Reduce heat and simmer, stirring occasionally, adding more water if the couscous becomes too dry, until the grains are tender, about 12 minutes. Season to taste with salt and pepper, and garnish with chopped pistachios.

Serves: 2 to 3
Prep Time: 5 minutes
Cooking Time: 20 minutes

CITRUS *and* HARVEST GRAINS SALAD

Although we serve this on greens, it is so grain-based that we think it belongs in the grains chapter. With or without the greens, this dish is tasty and brimming with healthful goodness.

VINAIGRETTE:

3 tablespoons Trader Joe's Orange Muscat Champagne Vinegar

2 teaspoons Dijon mustard

½ cup olive oil

salt and pepper

SALAD:

1 (4-ounce) bag mâche (or other soft lettuce)

1 cup Trader Joe's Harvest Grains Blend, cooked according to package directions

1 blood orange (or regular orange), peeled and sliced

1 ruby grapefruit, segmented

1 ripe avocado, sliced

¼ English cucumber, sliced

VEGETARIAN, VEGAN

FOR VINAIGRETTE: Whisk together the vinegar and mustard. While whisking vigorously, begin to drizzle in the olive oil, a little at a time. When the vinaigrette begins to thicken, add olive oil a little more at a time until all is incorporated. Taste on a leaf of lettuce, and adjust seasoning with salt and pepper.

FOR THE SALAD: Toss the greens with a little dressing and arrange on plates or a platter. Mound the cooked grains in the center of the platter, and drizzle on a little more dressing, reserving about two tablespoons of dressing. Arrange the citrus segments, avocado, and cucumber on the salad and drizzle with the remaining dressing.

Serves: 4
Prep Time: 5 minutes
Cooking Time: 15 minutes

QUINOA *with* GRILLED VEGETABLES *and* MINI-PEPPERS

While this nutty, fluffy wonder food might be newly available in the United States, there's nothing new about this ancient nutrient from high in the Andes. It's a great substitute for rice, and it's fun to say, too. KEEN-WHAAAA!

1 (16-ounce) box Trader Joe's Organic Quinoa

2 teaspoons olive oil or butter

6 Trader Joe's Minisweet Bell Peppers, sliced into rings

¼ cup Trader Joe's Grilled Vegetable Bruschetta (in a jar near the pastas)

salt and pepper, or Trader Joe's 21 Seasoning Salute

VEGETARIAN, VEGAN
(if olive oil is used)

Cook quinoa according to package directions. While the grain cooks, heat the butter or olive oil in a small sauté pan, and sauté the pepper rings over medium-high heat until tender, 3 to 4 minutes. Set aside. When quinoa is cooked, stir in ¼ cup Grilled Vegetable Bruschetta. Top with sautéed pepper rings. Season to taste with salt and pepper or 21 Seasoning Salute.

Serves: 4 to 6
Prep Time: 5 minutes
Cooking Time: 15 minutes

CHERRY RICE PILAF

This tasty side is a delight for the senses. The flavor of the dried cherries is deep, almost caramelly, and the walnuts add a toothsome crunch. The colors look great on a plate.

2 tablespoons butter

1 red onion, chopped

1 cup chopped celery

½ cup dried cherries

½ cup chopped walnuts

1 teaspoon dried thyme

3 cups cooked rice (white or brown)

salt and pepper

VEGETARIAN, GLUTEN-FREE

In a medium sauté pan, melt butter over medium heat. Sauté red onion, celery, cherries, walnuts, and thyme until tender, about 8 minutes. Combine with cooked rice, season with salt and pepper, and cook until heated through.

Serves: 2 to 4
Prep Time: 5 minutes
Cooking Time: 10 minutes

....

Cook extra rice for dinner the night before to give yourself a head start on this dish, or use precooked rice from the freezer aisle.

....

QUINOA-STUFFED GRILLED MUSHROOMS

This makes a great healthy lunch or a vegetarian entrée. The juicy grilled mushrooms are delicious, and the fluffy, slightly crunchy grains add nuttiness. And the cheese? Well, that's just for melty goodness!

½ cup Trader Joe's Quinoa, rinsed

1 cup water

6 Trader Joe's Stuffing Portabella Mushrooms

olive oil

3 slices of provolone cheese (or another cheese)

salt and pepper

2 teaspoons fresh thyme leaves

VEGETARIAN, GLUTEN-FREE

In a small saucepan, combine the water and quinoa and bring to a boil. Reduce heat to a simmer, cover, and cook quinoa, about 15 minutes. While the quinoa cooks, brush the mushrooms with a little olive oil and grill or sauté them in a separate pan over medium heat until tender, about 5 minutes per side. When the mushrooms are done, drape a half-slice of cheese over the hollow of each one and allow it to melt. Check the quinoa—the water should be absorbed and the quinoa softened. Fluff the grains and season to taste with salt and pepper. Spoon some quinoa on top of the cheese and sprinkle with thyme leaves.

Serves: 4 to 6
Prep Time: 5 minutes
Cooking Time: 15 minutes

• •
Try stirring in some Trader Joe's Corn and Chile Tomato-Less Salsa for added crunch, color, and zippy spice.
• •

ROASTED MUSHROOM POLENTA STACKS

These make a great vegetarian main dish or side dish. The Italian flavors are earthy and rustic, and the presentation is restaurant-worthy.

1 (18-ounce) roll Trader Joe's Organic Polenta, cut in ¼-inch rounds

4 Stuffing Portabella Mushrooms (or 2 portabellas)

1 tablespoon olive oil

4 ounces fresh mozzarella, cut into ¼-inch rounds

1 (24-ounce) jar Trader Giotto's Rustico Pomodoro Pasta Sauce (or another tasty sauce)

1 roasted red pepper, cut into strips

several fresh basil leaves, chiffonaded

salt and pepper

VEGETARIAN, GLUTEN-FREE

Preheat oven to 450°F. Place polenta rounds on a parchment-lined baking tray. Toss mushrooms with olive oil and season with salt and pepper. Place on the baking tray and roast until mushrooms are tender, about 10 minutes. Slice into strips. Place a warmed polenta round on each plate and top with a slice of mozzarella and a dollop of pasta sauce. Drape some mushroom strips across the top and then some red pepper strips. Top with chiffonaded basil.

Serves: 4
Prep Time: 10 minutes
Cooking Time: 10 minutes

YA YA CHERIE'S QUICK and DIRTY JAMBALAYA

I'm not claimin' it's strictly authentic, y'all—but if you want a tasty bowl of rice and goodness, give this a whirl.

2 tablespoons butter

2 tablespoons grapeseed oil

1 onion, chopped

1 green bell pepper, chopped

2 ribs celery, chopped

3 green onions, chopped

3 cubes frozen crushed garlic

1 jalapeño, chopped

1 teaspoon red chile pepper flakes, crushed

¼ teaspoon dried thyme

1 (12.8-ounce) package Trader Joe's Smoked Andouille Chicken Sausage, sliced ½-inch thick

2 cups chicken broth

½ cup white wine

1 (15-ounce) can chopped tomatoes in juice

3 cups long grain white rice

1 pound raw medium shrimp, peeled

1 cup Trader Joe's Just Chicken (optional)

GLUTEN-FREE

In a large sauté pan, melt the butter and oil over medium-high heat until sizzling. Add the "holy trinity" (the onion, bell pepper, and celery) and sauté until fragrant, about 3 minutes. Add the green onions, garlic, and jalapeño, and sauté 3 minutes. Add crushed red chile pepper flakes and thyme and sauté until vegetables are tender, about 5 to 7 more minutes. Add the sliced sausage, chicken broth, wine, and tomatoes, and bring to a boil. Stir in the rice and bring back to the boil. Reduce heat to low, cover, and simmer 20 minutes. Remove the lid, stir the rice, and add the shrimp. (If using Just Chicken, add it now.) Cover the pan, remove from heat, and let stand 10 minutes. Uncover and check shrimp—if they are cooked through, the dish is finished. If not, tuck them into the rice and cover the pan for 5 more minutes.

Serves: 6

Prep Time: 15 minutes

Cooking Time: 45 minutes

CHAMPAGNE-SAFFRON RISOTTO

I confess that I always have shrimp and puff pastry in my freezer, and I always have Champagne in my fridge. That means I'm party-ready, 24-7. This recipe combines the luxury of saffron, the world's most costly spice, and creamy, broth-plumped rice grains.

1 large pinch Trader Joe's Spanish Saffron threads

5 cups chicken, beef, or vegetable broth, kept warm

4 tablespoons butter, divided

1 shallot, diced

1 cup Arborio rice

½ cup Champagne (or dry white wine)

salt and white pepper

grated Parmigiano-Reggiano

VEGETARIAN
(if vegetable broth is used)

Crumble and soak the saffron in about ½ cup of the broth. Set aside. In a large sauté pan, melt half the butter and sauté the diced shallots over medium-high heat until fragrant, 3 to 4 minutes. Add the rice and stir gently to coat the grains with the butter. When the grains are glistening, add the Champagne and stir until it is nearly gone. Begin to add broth, a ladleful at a time, starting with the saffron soaking liquid. Stir gently until the rice has absorbed the broth almost entirely, then add another ladleful of broth. Repeat, one ladleful at a time, stirring continuously, until all the broth is used. From the first addition of the broth, the risotto will take approximately 18 minutes to achieve the proper texture.

After about 15 minutes, season the risotto lightly with salt and white pepper, and then begin tasting a grain or two of rice until the desired texture is achieved. (The rice should maintain a slight resistance at the center.) When the rice has just slightly more resistance than you'd like the finished dish to have, add one more ladleful of stock and turn heat to very low. Add the remaining butter and about ½ cup of grated cheese and stir very gently to incorporate the ingredients. Adjust seasonings with salt and white pepper and serve.

Serves: 4
Prep Time: 10 minutes
Cooking Time: 30 minutes

RED, WHITE, and BLUE FIRECRACKER POTATO SALAD

Perfect for Bastille Day, Fourth of July, or any summer celebration calling for red, white, and blue (or bleu)!

1 pound Trader Joe's Potato Medley, or a mixture of red, white, and blue (purple) boiling potatoes, cut into 1-inch cubes

½ cup crème fraîche

¼ cup Trader Joe's Bold and Smoky Kansas City-Style Barbecue Sauce

4 green onions, chopped

½ red onion, chopped

salt and pepper

VEGETARIAN, GLUTEN-FREE

Bring a large pot of lightly salted water to a boil. Add potatoes and cook until a skewer penetrates easily but potatoes retain a slight firmness. Drain. Combine crème fraîche and barbecue sauce. Add to warm potatoes and toss to combine. Add chopped green and red onions, toss again, and season to taste with salt and pepper. Serve at room temperature or chilled.

Serves: 4
Prep Time: 10 minutes
Cooking Time: 15 minutes

SAFFRON POTATOES and PANCETTA

These are absolutely gorgeous and full of flavor. Another great tapa or a side dish perfect for roast chicken or fish.

½ pound fingerling potatoes, halved lengthwise

pinch of saffron

2 teaspoons balsamic vinegar

1 shallot, minced

2 tablespoons crème fraîche

½ cup chopped pancetta

salt and pepper

2 tablespoons Italian parsley, chopped

GLUTEN-FREE

Place potatoes and saffron in a medium saucepan and cover with water. Bring to a boil, reduce heat, and simmer until tender, about 15 minutes. Drain the potatoes and toss with balsamic vinegar. In a medium bowl, mix minced shallot, crème fraîche, and pancetta. Toss in the slightly cooled potatoes and adjust seasoning with salt and pepper. Garnish with parsley.

Serves: 2 as a side dish, 4 as a tapa
Prep Time: 5 minutes
Cooking Time: 20 minutes

Chapter 5

POULTRY

When time is tight, chicken or turkey is what's for dinner, chez moi. It's fast and easy on the wallet, and cooking is a virtual no-brainer. What more could you ask from the poultry case? You can take that poultry in so many flavor directions—it's the meat equivalent of tofu. Gussied up with curry sauce, barbecue sauce, pesto, or salsa, it's all good.

Even if I'm pressed for time, I generally reach for bone-in chicken pieces because they yield so much more flavor than their boneless, skinless counterparts. Keeping the meat on the bone also helps keep the meat from drying out. (If you doubt that there's a big difference in flavor, just think of the ingredients in a good pot of chicken broth—it's 90 percent bones, a few veggies, and water, and yet you get such a rich, chicken-y flavor after some simmering. It's the bones, baby!)

But boneless poultry also has its place in my kitchen. Slap a package of turkey cutlets in my cart and I can have a plate of Turkey with Green Chile Sauce on the table in the time it takes to cook the rice to go with it. And chicken thighs, even boneless, pack a flavor wallop. Sauté or stir-fry them with a couple handfuls of shredded carrots and baby squashes from the fresh produce section or with a bagful of frozen vegetables in sauce, and dinner doesn't get much quicker. At my Joe's, the poultry case is next to the refrigerated case that houses the salsas and pestos. Grab a package of poultry, pick a container from that section, and experiment with pairing them up. Hummus with some roasted chicken in a pita? Yes, please!

One of the things I really appreciate about Trader Joe's is that each section of the store is relatively small compared to a conventional grocery store, and especially compared to the big box stores. What that means to me is that they are constantly replenishing the shelves and refrigerated cases. This frequent turnover ensures a fresher product in the poultry case, and that means more delicious and healthful dishes on your table.

Kosher, free-range, or organic poultry—Trader Joe's has them all, and at far better prices than some of the fancy-schmancy grocery emporia. So grab a package of white or dark meat, or a whole roaster, and get ready to have a terrific TJ's meal.

TURKEY with GREEN CHILE SAUCE

Creamy, spicy goodness takes turkey to a new level. This is one of my favorite recipes from recent TJ's cooking classes. Serve with roasted butternut squash and brown rice for a warming autumn dinner.

1 pound turkey cutlets

1 tablespoon olive oil

3 cubes frozen crushed garlic

1 cup Blackthorn Fermented Cider or dry white wine

2 tablespoons Trader Joe's Hatch Valley Fire-Roasted Diced Green Chiles

½ cup ripe Brie, rind removed

salt and pepper

GLUTEN-FREE

Season the turkey cutlets with salt and pepper. In a medium sauté pan, heat the olive oil and sauté the garlic over medium heat for 2 to 3 minutes, until fragrant. Add the turkey cutlets in a single layer and cook until barely seared on both sides, about 2 minutes. (Work in batches, if necessary.) Remove to a platter. Add the hard cider or wine to the pan and bring to a boil. Reduce heat and simmer until the cider is reduced by half, about 5 minutes. Return the cutlets to the pan and cook through. Remove again to the serving platter and keep warm. Add the chopped chiles and Brie to the sauté pan and simmer until cheese melts and sauce is thickened. Pour over cutlets and serve.

Serves: 4
Prep Time: 5 minutes
Cooking Time: 15 minutes

BLACK PEPPER CHICKEN with WINTER SQUASH

A splash of color to perk up a gray day, this dish is zingy with spice from the Black Pepper Sauce.

1 tablespoon olive oil

4 chicken thighs (bone in, skin on)

1 red onion, thinly sliced

2 cubes frozen crushed garlic

1 pound acorn squash or butternut squash cubes

1 cup dry white wine

1 tube Trader Joe's chicken Savory Broth concentrate

½ (10-ounce) bottle Trader Joe's Black Pepper Sauce

Preheat oven to 400°F. Heat the olive oil in a medium sauté pan. Place the chicken thighs in the pan, skin-side down, and brown the chicken over medium-high heat until skin is golden, about 7 minutes. Turn chicken, and cook 3 to 4 minutes on the other side. Remove chicken to a platter. Pour off all but about a tablespoon of the fat. Sauté the sliced onion until softened, about 3 minutes. Add the garlic and sauté until fragrant, 1 to 2 minutes. Add the squash cubes and sauté about 5 minutes. Pour in the wine and the contents of the chicken broth tube, and bring to a boil. Reduce heat and simmer 5 minutes. Add about ⅓ cup of the Black Pepper Sauce and stir to combine. Place chicken thighs on top of the vegetables and brush with the remaining sauce. Bake for 20 to 25 minutes, until chicken is cooked through.

Serves: 4

Prep Time: 5 minutes

Cooking Time: less than an hour

GENERAL TSAO CHICKEN WRAPS

Kids love to put these together, and they are as healthful as they are tangy-crunchy-good.

1 tablespoon grapeseed or canola oil

½ pound boneless chicken (thighs, breasts or a combination), coarsely chopped

about ¼ cup Trader Joe's General Tsao Stir-Fry Sauce

½ (10-ounce) bag shredded carrots

1 head large, sturdy lettuce, like romaine

In a medium sauté pan, heat the oil and sauté the chicken over medium-high heat until cooked through. (The time will depend on how small the chicken pieces are.) With a knife or in a food processor, chop the cooked chicken finely. Stir in General Tsao sauce until the mixture is moist but not too drippy. Add shredded carrots and bundle into lettuce leaves.

Serves: 4
Prep Time: 5 minutes
Cooking Time: less than 10 minutes

HOT TODDY CHICKEN

Good for what ails ya!

2 pounds chicken thighs

2 teaspoons olive oil

1 tube Trader Joe's chicken Savory Broth concentrate

½ cup water

½ cup orange marmalade

2 tablespoons whiskey

1 tablespoon honey

pinch of red chile pepper flakes

salt and pepper

GLUTEN-FREE

Season the chicken thighs with salt and pepper. Heat the oil in a large sauté pan over medium-high heat and brown the chicken on both sides, in batches. When all chicken is browned, return it to the pan and pour in the concentrated chicken broth and water. Cover and simmer over low heat (10 minutes for boneless thighs, 25 for bone-in). Combine the marmalade, whiskey, honey, and red chile pepper flakes and pour into the pan, stirring to combine with the pan liquid. Simmer until sauce is thickened and thighs are well-coated and cooked through.

Serves: 4 to 6
Prep Time: 15 minutes
Cooking Time: less than 45 minutes

PESTO CHICKEN SALAD

 While not a traditional Italian dish, this chicken salad has the flavors of a Ligurian summer day. Sip a glass of Pinot Grigio and dream of the Mediterranean.

¼ cup Trader Giotto's Pesto alla Genovese (in the refrigerated case)

3 tablespoons red wine vinegar

2 tablespoons olive oil

1½ cup Trader Joe's Just Chicken (or cooked chicken), coarsely chopped

1 (7-ounce) bag arugula or mixed baby greens

¼ English cucumber, chopped

½ cup shredded carrots

½ red onion, chopped

¼ cup toasted pine nuts

salt and pepper

GLUTEN-FREE

Whisk together the pesto, vinegar, and olive oil. Season to taste with salt and pepper. Toss the chicken with half the pesto mixture. In a large bowl, combine the arugula (or mixed greens), chopped cucumber, carrots, and red onion, and dress with the remaining pesto mixture. Adjust seasoning to taste. Arrange on a platter and top with the chicken. Sprinkle pine nuts over the salad.

Serves: 2 to 4
Prep Time: 10 minutes
Cooking Time: none

PROSCIUTTO TURKEY TENDERLOIN *with* FINGERLINGS

This one is a keeper—a quick zap in the microwave gets the vegetables going quickly, then they finish roasting along with the turkey for a savory finale.

1 (1-pound) package fingerling potatoes, halved (or 1 pound boiling potatoes, cut in quarters)

1 (12-ounce) package Trader Joe's Sweet Potato Spears

1 to 2 tablespoons olive oil

2 cubes frozen crushed garlic

3 tablespoons maple syrup

sprinkle of red chile pepper flakes

2 turkey tenderloins (or pork tenderloins)

4 ounces of sliced prosciutto

GLUTEN-FREE

Preheat oven to 425°F. Combine the potatoes and sweet potato spears in an ovenproof and microwaveable casserole and drizzle with olive oil. Microwave 4 minutes. Combine the garlic, maple syrup, and a sprinkle of red chile pepper flakes. Reserve about 1 tablespoon of this mixture and rub the rest on the turkey (or pork) tenderloins. Wrap the tenderloin in prosciutto. Place in the casserole on top of the potatoes. Roast 25 minutes. Drizzle with the remaining maple syrup mixture and roast until the internal temperature of the tenderloins is 150°F on a meat thermometer. Let the tenderloin rest 5 to 10 minutes before carving.

Serves: 4 to 6
Prep Time: 10 minutes
Cooking Time: 30 minutes

• •
Microwaving the vegetables speeds up the prep, but if you prefer, you can roast the potatoes and sweet potato spears in the oven for about 20 minutes before adding the turkey.
• •

CHAMPAGNE CHICKEN *with* CHAMPIGNONS

Simple enough for a weeknight, elegant enough for company, this chicken dish is rich and flavorful. Serve over rice or pasta, with haricots verts (French green beans) or roasted asparagus.

1 tablespoon butter

1½ pounds boneless chicken breasts or thighs

2 cubes frozen crushed garlic

2 shallots, thinly sliced

6 ounces mushrooms, thinly sliced

¾ cup Champagne or sparkling wine

½ to ¾ cup heavy cream

salt and white pepper

GLUTEN-FREE

In a large sauté pan, heat the butter over medium heat and sauté the chicken until it loses its pink color, about 4 minutes on each side. Add the garlic and shallots to the pan, and sauté until shallots are softened, about 4 minutes. Add the mushrooms and Champagne (it will fizz up, then subside) and season lightly with salt and white pepper. Cover the pan and simmer, turning chicken once, 10 to 15 minutes, until chicken is cooked through. Remove chicken to a warm platter. Increase heat to high and reduce cooking liquid until about ¼ cup remains. Add the cream and reduce by half, about 4 minutes. Pour the sauce over the chicken on the platter and serve.

Serves: 4
Prep Time: 10 minutes
Cooking Time: 30 minutes

CHICKEN and PEPPERS in CRÈME SAUCE

The colorful peppers make this dish pop on the plate. The flavors are mellow and rich, without a lot of fat.

1 pound chicken tenders, or breasts cut into strips

2 tablespoons olive oil

1 pint Trader Joe's Minisweet Bell Peppers, sliced into strips

⅓ cup dry white wine

1 tablespoon Dijon mustard

¾ cup water

1 tube Trader Joe's chicken Savory Broth concentrate

2 tablespoons crème fraîche (or cream)

salt and pepper

GLUTEN-FREE

Season chicken tenders with salt and pepper. In a large sauté pan, heat the olive oil over medium-high heat and sauté the tenders until they are no longer pink, about 5 minutes. Add the mini-pepper strips and sauté 3 to 4 minutes more, until peppers are softened. Remove chicken and peppers to a serving platter. Deglaze the pan with the white wine, gently loosening the browned bits of food with a wooden spoon or spatula, and simmer 2 to 3 minutes, until wine is reduced to about a tablespoon. Add the mustard, water, and chicken broth concentrate, and simmer 2 to 3 minutes, until the liquid is slightly reduced. Add the crème fraîche and simmer a moment to warm. Return the chicken and peppers to the pan and simmer until warm and cooked through. Adjust seasonings to taste with salt and pepper.

Serves: 4
Prep Time: 5 minutes
Cooking Time: 20 minutes

ASIAN-STYLE CHICKEN with SESAME NUTS

Another take-out dish without the carton. Don't be put off by the ingredient list—this goes together fast and tastes terrific.

2 teaspoons olive oil

1 pound boneless chicken (thighs, breasts, or both), cut into bite-sized pieces

3 tablespoons soy sauce

2 tablespoons dry sherry

2 tablespoons tangerine or orange juice

1 teaspoon sugar

1 teaspoon Trader Joe's Crushed Ginger (in a jar) or minced fresh ginger

½ teaspoon crushed red chile pepper flakes

1 tablespoon water

2 teaspoons cornstarch

¼ cup julienned carrots (optional)

½ cup Trader Joe's Hot and Sweet Sesame Nuts (or use ½ cup Tsao Nuts from the Appetizer chapter)

¼ cup sliced green onions

3 cups cooked rice

In a large sauté pan, heat the oil over medium-high heat and sauté the chicken just until it loses its raw appearance, about 5 minutes. Combine the soy sauce, sherry, tangerine or orange juice, sugar, crushed ginger, and crushed red chile pepper flakes, and pour into the sauté pan. Bring to a boil, reduce heat, and simmer until chicken is just cooked through, about 5 more minutes. Combine the water and cornstarch, stirring to incorporate well. Pour into the sauté pan and cook until sauce thickens, 1 to 2 minutes. Add carrots (if using) and stir to warm through. Adjust seasoning to taste with more soy sauce and red chile pepper flakes. Stir in Hot and Sweet Sesame Nuts. Garnish with green onions and serve over rice.

Serves: 4
Prep Time: 10 minutes
Cooking Time: 15 minutes

CHICKEN *with* OLIVES

This dish is great as a main course or as a tapa. The Spanish-influenced ingredients bring a sunny flavor to the chicken.

2 pounds chicken thighs (bone in, skin on)

1 tablespoon olive oil

½ teaspoon ground cumin

1 red onion, thinly sliced

4 cubes frozen crushed garlic

½ cup orange juice

juice of ½ lemon

1 cup green olives (pitted or not)

salt and pepper

GLUTEN-FREE

Lightly season the thighs with salt and pepper. Heat the olive oil in a large sauté pan over high heat and brown the chicken in batches, removing pieces to a platter as they are browned. When all chicken is browned (but not cooked through), pour off all but 1 tablespoon of accumulated juices. Add the cumin and toast until aromatic, 1 to 2 minutes. Add the onion and sauté 5 minutes, until softened. Add garlic and sauté 3 to 4 minutes, until fragrant. Add the orange and lemon juice and return the chicken to the pan. Add the olives, cover the pan, and adjust heat to medium. Simmer, covered, another 10 to 15 minutes, until the chicken is cooked through.

Serves: 4
Prep Time: 5 minutes
Cooking Time: 30 minutes

MAPLE MUSTARD CHICKEN

A great pantry meal, this takes just moments to make and then hangs out in the oven while you pull the rest of the meal together. A quick salad and maybe some Trader Joe's Harvest Grains Blend, and you are good to go!

½ cup Dijon mustard

¼ cup maple syrup

1 tablespoon rice vinegar

1½ pounds boneless chicken thighs

salt and pepper

Preheat oven to 450°F. Combine the mustard, maple syrup, and rice vinegar. Place the chicken in a single layer in an ovenproof casserole, and season with salt and pepper. Pour the mustard-maple syrup mixture over the chicken, turning to coat. Roast until interior of chicken thighs reach 155°F on a meat thermometer, about 20 minutes. Let the chicken rest 5 minutes before serving.

Serves: 4 to 6
Prep Time: 5 minutes
Cooking Time: 20 minutes

PROSCIUTTO-WRAPPED CHICKEN

This comes together fast, but the big flavor lingers.

**6 chicken thighs
(bone in, skin on)**

6 slices prosciutto

1 tablespoon olive oil

½ cup white wine

**1 tube Trader Joe's chicken
Savory Broth concentrate**

1 tablespoon balsamic vinegar

1 tablespoon butter

**salt and freshly ground
black pepper**

GLUTEN-FREE

Season chicken thighs with freshly ground black pepper. Place each chicken thigh on top of a piece of prosciutto and wrap the ends up over the sides of the chicken. Heat the oil in a medium sauté pan and place the chicken thighs in a single layer, prosciutto-side down. Cook over medium heat, 10 to 15 minutes, until prosciutto is nicely crisp. Turn the pieces over and cook on the other side until cooked through, 10 to 15 minutes more. Remove the thighs to a serving platter. Drain off all but 1 tablespoon of fat and deglaze the pan with the white wine, bringing it to a boil and gently loosening the bits of food with a spoon or spatula. Add the concentrated chicken broth and simmer 2 minutes. Swirl in the balsamic vinegar and butter, and season to taste with salt and pepper. Place a spoonful of the sauce on each plate and place a thigh on each plate, prosciutto-side up.

Serves: 6
Prep Time: 10 minutes
Cooking Time: 30 minutes

Chapter 6

BEEF AND LAMB

"Beef. It's what's for dinner." Remember that ad campaign? There are plenty of times when it's still true. Whether you're a confirmed beefaholic or cutting back on the red stuff, if you partake at all, Trader Joe's has a small but mighty selection of cuts to delight your palate and your pocket. Some of the beef is grass-fed, some is Black Angus, and all of it is fresh and ready to grill, broil, or braise when you need to "get your beef on." From down-home tri-tip steaks and roasts, both great for barbecuing, to upscale cuts like New York strips and filet mignon, there's something to delight any carnivore. My favorite cut? It's gotta be a rib-eye—the butcher's cut—full of great beef flavor.

I'm somewhat of a purist when it comes to steaks—I don't eat them often, but when I decide to partake, I really want to taste the flavor of the meat itself. So generally, I'll salt and pepper the meat (or give it a Trader Joe's 21 Seasoning Salute!) and grill it on the rare side. If I'm feeling particularly luxe, I'll slice a pat of compound butter on the sizzling meat. Maybe Maître d'Hotel butter or Port and Gorgonzola butter—there are so many flavor combinations that are great with beef. If I'm feeling both luxe and lazy, a handful of crumbled Gorgonzola or Maytag blue cheese scattered on the steak as soon as it leaves the grill makes a decadent instant sauce. This is not to say I'm anti-marinade. There are several marinated cuts in the Trader Joe's meat case that I rely on for quick and yummy meals. The chipotle-marinated flat iron steak combines two of my favorite flavors. A chipotle is a dried, smoked jalapeño that delivers a slightly sweet, smoky kiss of heat. The flat iron steak, which is sometimes hard to find, has a very rich, beefy flavor. Cook it rare for best effect. You don't need a huge serving of this luscious meat to get full beef impact.

Trader Joe's is the only place nearby where I can find lamb in any fashion other than leg or chops. We Americans have been conditioned to be somewhat lamb-phobic, and that's a real shame. I believe it's the fat that sometimes gives lamb a gamey taste, and none of the lamb at Trader Joe's is fatty. I love the lamb loins, which cook up so quickly and yield such tender, flavorful morsels. A lightning-quick sear or sauté and a super-fast pan sauce, and dinner's served.

The cuts available vary by season and from store to store. But no matter which Joe's I visit, if red meat is on the menu, I can always find something that will suit the occasion. Maybe they should modify that ad—"Beef or lamb. They're what's for dinner!"

TRI-TIP ASADA with HEIRLOOM TOMATOES

As gorgeous as it is delicious, this dish puts a summer evening on the calendar any time of year.

1 Trader Joe's Carne Asada Autentica tri-tip steak (about 1½ pounds)

4 large or 8 small heirloom tomatoes

1 ripe avocado

½ red onion

¼ to ½ cup Trader Ming's Sesame Soy Vinaigrette

Heat a grill to high heat and sear the tri-tip on both sides. Reduce heat to medium and cover the grill. Cook until rare, or until the internal heat registers 130°F on a meat thermometer. (If cooking on a charcoal grill, mound the coals on one side and, after the tri-tip is seared, move it to the area without coals. Cover the grill so the meat will cook over indirect heat). Let the meat rest at least 10 minutes before slicing thinly. Slice tomatoes and arrange on a platter. Slice the avocado and red onion and arrange along the edges of the platter. Dress lightly with the vinaigrette and arrange the sliced tri-tip in the center.

Serves: 4 to 6
Prep Time: 10 minutes
Cooking Time: less than 30 minutes

MAUI BEEF on COCONUT RICE with MACADAMIA NUTS and BASIL

 Macadamia nuts lend a great crunch, and the mango and basil make the dish "pop" on the platter.

1 cup light coconut milk

1 cup water
(or vegetable or chicken broth)

1 cup raw Trader Joe's Thai
Jasmine Rice or basmati rice
(or use frozen or precooked rice
and omit water or broth)

salt

¼ cup macadamia nuts, chopped

handful of fresh basil leaves,
chiffonaded

1 to 1½ pounds Trader Joe's
Hawaiian Style Maui Beef
Boneless Short Ribs

½ fresh mango, sliced,
or ½ package presliced mango,
for garnish

In a medium saucepan, bring the coconut milk and water (or broth) to a boil. Stir in the rice and bring the liquid back to a boil. Reduce heat to very low, cover, and cook with lid on for 15 minutes. Remove from heat, leaving lid on, and let stand 5 minutes. Remove lid, fluff the rice, and season with a little salt. Stir in the chopped nuts. Just before serving, sprinkle with the basil. Grill or broil short ribs 3 to 5 minutes per side. Serve the grilled or broiled beef strips on top of the rice, garnished with mango slices.

Serves: 4 to 6

Prep Time: 10 minutes

Cooking Time: 25 minutes

• •

If you love the flavor of coconut, increase the amount of coconut milk to 1½ cups and add ½ cup of water (in place of the 1 cup water or stock) to make the rice.

• •

PEPPERED BEEF and RICE STICKS

Texture, color, and crunch all come together in this recipe in a yummy tangle of silky noodles and tender beef strips. A treat for the eyes and the taste buds.

¾ to 1 pound tender beef steaks (boneless rib-eye, tenderloin, or other cut), sliced into strips

1 tablespoon olive oil

coarsely ground black pepper

½ (13.2-ounce) package Trader Joe's Rice Sticks (Thai pasta)

1 cup baby spinach leaves

½ cup shredded carrots

¼ English cucumber, cut into thin strips

1 tablespoon red wine vinegar

1 tablespoon soy sauce

2 tablespoons sesame oil

2 green onions, chopped

Bring a pot of water to a boil for the rice sticks. Brush the steak strips with olive oil and sprinkle with the pepper. Heat a sauté pan and sauté the steak strips over medium-high heat for 2 to 3 minutes, until cooked but rare. Remove to a warm platter. Cook the rice sticks until tender, 6 to 8 minutes. Before you drain the noodles, place the spinach leaves and shredded carrots in the bottom of a colander. When the rice sticks are cooked, drain them over the vegetables in the colander. The hot water will wilt the raw vegetables slightly. Toss the rice sticks with the cucumber, red wine vinegar, soy sauce, and sesame oil. Add the beef and garnish with green onions.

Serves: 4
Prep Time: 10 minutes
Cooking Time: 15 minutes

. . . .

The rice sticks are stocked regionally. If you can't locate them, use a long, thin pasta of your choice, or omit the noodles entirely. Use hot water to wilt the vegetables and then toss them with the dressing.

. . . .

CHIPOTLE FLAT IRON STEAK SALAD with ROASTED BABY ARTICHOKES

 I love to serve this in winter because the artichoke hearts and mushrooms bring an earthiness that's so welcome when the temperature drops.

1 container (about 12) baby artichokes, or 1 (16-ounce) bag frozen artichoke hearts, thawed

1 (1 to 1½ pound) Trader Joe's Flat Iron Beef Chuck Steak Seasoned in a Chipotle Pepper BBQ Sauce

1 (8-ounce) container crimini mushrooms, wiped clean

1 (1-pint) container cherry tomatoes or grape tomatoes

3 cubes frozen crushed garlic

1 (5-ounce) bag baby greens or romaine lettuce, shredded

1 tablespoon Dijon mustard

2 tablespoons red wine vinegar

⅓ cup olive oil, plus more to drizzle over artichokes and mushrooms

shaved Parmesan cheese (optional)

salt and pepper

Preheat oven to 400°F. Trim outer leaves and tips of remaining leaves from baby artichokes. Toss the artichokes with a little olive oil. Place on a baking sheet in a single layer and season with salt and pepper. Roast until artichokes are nearly tender, about 15 minutes. While vegetables roast, in a medium ovenproof sauté pan, sear the steak well on both sides and place the pan in the oven for about 8 minutes, until steak is cooked to desired degree of doneness. Let steak rest 5 minutes before slicing into thin strips.

Meanwhile, toss the mushrooms with a little more olive oil and add the garlic cubes, crushing the cubes to incorporate them. Add the garlic-mushroom mixture to the baking sheet with the artichokes and season with a little more salt and pepper. Roast until tender, 8 to 10 minutes. (If using defrosted artichoke hearts, roast all the vegetables together for about 10 minutes.)

Arrange the greens on a platter and top with roasted vegetables, the tomatoes, and the thinly sliced steak. Whisk together the mustard and red wine vinegar and then slowly stream in the oil, whisking constantly. Add any meat juices that have accumulated to the dressing, then season it to taste with salt and pepper and drizzle over the salad. Garnish with shaved Parmesan cheese, if desired.

If you prefer your tomatoes roasted, add them with the mushrooms, olive oil, and garlic.

BOURBON-BALSAMIC BEEF

Another pantry dish (assuming you keep bourbon in your pantry!) that goes together quickly and packs a punch of flavor.

¼ **cup bourbon**

¼ **cup balsamic vinegar**

¼ **cup brown sugar**

2 tablespoons Trader Joe's Crushed Ginger (in a jar) or minced fresh ginger

1½ pounds flank steak

Place all ingredients in a resealable plastic bag. Marinate as little as 20 minutes or as long as overnight. Grill or broil the steak to desired doneness, turning once, then slice against the grain (or slice the raw beef and sauté the strips with a little olive oil over medium-high heat.)

Serves: 4 to 6

Prep Time: 5 minutes, plus 20 minutes or more to marinate the steaks

Cooking Time: 10 to 15 minutes

Serve with Green Beans with Red Onion and Creamy Feta Dressing, with roasted potatoes, or over salad greens.

STEAK *and* GREEN BEAN SALAD *with* BLUE CHEESE

We really do eat with our eyes first, and the look of this salad starts my tummy rumbling. A casual tumble of steak strips (make mine quite rare, please), brightly colored beans, and lush, ripe tomatoes makes a great presentation. This no-greens, meaty salad is great for evenings when you grill, or even the night after using leftover steak.

DRESSING:

2 tablespoons balsamic vinegar

1 tablespoon Dijon mustard

¼ cup olive oil

¼ cup grapeseed or canola oil

½ pound green beans, cooked until crisp-tender

1 pound rare grilled steak (rib-eye, skirt, sirloin, or whatever you like), sliced in strips

1 gorgeous tomato, cut in eighths

2 ounces firm blue cheese

salt and freshly ground black pepper

Make dressing by whisking together the vinegar and mustard, then whisking in the oils. Arrange the green beans and steak strips on a platter, and garnish with the tomato wedges. Season lightly with salt and freshly ground black pepper. Crumble the blue cheese evenly over the top, add the salad dressing, and toss to combine.

Serves: 4

Prep Time: 10 minutes

Cooking Time: less than 10 minutes

• •

A combination of green and yellow beans is pretty in this dish, too. Make sure the beans are young and tender, not "woody."

• •

I like Danish blue cheese for this dish—Gorgonzola and Roquefort can be too soft to crumble easily. Of course, you can take advantage of the pre-crumbled blue cheeses TJ's carries. I just like to lick my fingers after I crumble the cheese!

• •

SIRLOIN SALAD with a LATIN KICK

This can be on the table in about 10 minutes, and it sure beats the other type of "fast food"!

1 (5-ounce) bag of Trader Joe's Baby Spring Mix (or other lettuce mix)

1 tablespoon olive oil

½ package Trader Joe's Very Thinly Sliced Sirloin (or about ¾ pound of another tender beef, such as sirloin or New York, thinly sliced)

1 tablespoon balsamic vinegar

about ½ cup Trader Joe's Corn and Chile Tomato-Less Salsa

1 ripe avocado, sliced

salt and pepper

GLUTEN-FREE

Arrange lettuce on a platter. Heat the olive oil in a large sauté pan and sauté the sirloin over medium-high heat until rare. Add the balsamic vinegar and heat through. Season to taste with salt and pepper and place on top of the greens. Spoon some of the corn salsa over the salad and top with avocado slices.

Serves: 4
Prep Time: 5 minutes
Cooking Time: 10 minutes

THAI BEEF SALAD

Improvise with other vegetables. Multicolored bell pepper strips, blanched snow peas, or mushrooms are all delicious and pretty in this salad as well.

1½ to 2 pounds flank steak

1 cup fresh lime juice, divided

½ cup soy sauce, divided

1 jalapeño, minced

1 tablespoon brown sugar

2 ripe tomatoes, cut in eighths

1 English cucumber, thinly sliced

1 red onion, thinly sliced

1 cup shredded carrots

1 cup fresh basil or mint leaves

Marinate flank steak in ½ cup lime juice and ¼ cup soy sauce for 4 hours or overnight.

Toss vegetables with remaining lime juice, soy sauce, jalapeño, and sugar. Grill steak over hot coals, broil, or sauté over high heat for 3 to 5 minutes per side. Let stand 5 to 10 minutes, then slice thinly across the grain. Combine beef and vegetables, tossing well. Add basil or mint leaves, toss again, and serve.

Serves: 4 to 6
Prep Time: 15 minutes, plus marinating time
Cooking Time: 10 minutes

FAT TIRE FLAMMADE

Personally, I'm more of a wine girl than a beer girl. But while wine would work well in this recipe, the beer brings a hearty richness to this dish that's really terrific!

1 tablespoon olive oil

1½ pounds Trader Joe's Black Angus Steak Tips (or New York Strip steak or top sirloin filet, cut into bite-sized chunks)

1 (8-ounce) bag peeled cipollini onions, cut in half

3 cubes frozen crushed garlic

½ (16-ounce) bag peeled baby carrots

2 tablespoons tomato paste

1 (16-ounce) bag fingerling potatoes, halved

2 tubes Trader Joe's beef Savory Broth concentrate

1 (12-ounce) Fat Tire beer

salt and pepper

In a medium sauté pan, heat the oil and brown the beef cubes in batches over medium-high heat. As beef is browned, remove to a plate; continue until all meat is browned. In the same pan, sauté the cipollini onions and garlic cubes until aromatic, about 2 minutes. Add the carrots and tomato paste and sauté 3 minutes, until tomato paste is caramelized. Add the potatoes and the browned meat, and pour the contents of the beef concentrate tubes over the top. Add the beer and stir to incorporate. Season with salt and pepper and bring to a boil. Reduce heat, cover, and simmer until beef and vegetables are tender, 30 to 45 minutes.

Serves: 4
Prep Time: 15 minutes
Cooking Time: about 1 hour

• •

If you have extra time, you can use Trader Joe's Lean Beef Stew Meat. It will take about twice as long to simmer to tenderness, but the flavor will be great.

• •

COMPOUND BUTTERS for STEAK

About twice a year, I need a good, rare steak, with all the fixin's—sautéed mushrooms, caramelized onions, the whole nine yards. Having a few of these simple, yet tremendously flavorful, compound butters stashed in the freezer makes the whole thing come together in the time it takes to heat the grill. Any of these will be great atop a grilled sirloin, filet, or (my favorite) rib-eye.

PORT AND GORGONZOLA BUTTER

4 ounces (1 stick) unsalted butter, at room temperature

4 ounces Gorgonzola (or other blue cheese), crumbled

1 tablespoon port

¼ cup chopped walnuts (optional)

salt and pepper

Combine all the ingredients in a food processor or with a mixer. Season to taste with salt and pepper. Wrap in parchment or plastic wrap and freeze. Slice off thin slices to serve on top of hot, grilled steaks.

FLAVOR VARIATIONS Follow the instructions for the Gorgonzola butter with each of the following flavorings:

LEMON CAPER BUTTER

4 ounces (1 stick) unsalted butter, at room temperature

zest and juice of 1 lemon

2 tablespoons capers

2 teaspoons Dijon mustard

GARLIC ROSEMARY BUTTER

4 ounces (1 stick) unsalted butter, at room temperature

2 tablespoons finely chopped rosemary

3 cubes frozen crushed garlic

TAPENADE BUTTER

4 ounces (1 stick) unsalted butter, at room temperature

¼ cup Trader Joe's green Olive Tapenade (or any other tapenade)

MAITRE D'HOTEL BUTTER

4 ounces (1 stick) unsalted butter, at room temperature

2 anchovies

2 tablespoons Italian parsley

zest and juice of 1 lemon

THYME BUTTER

4 ounces (1 stick) unsalted butter, at room temperature

1 shallot, finely minced

2 cubes frozen crushed garlic

2 teaspoons fresh thyme leaves

....

Once these butters are stashed in the freezer, they make great instant sauces for more than just steak. Try some slices stirred into white or brown rice, on top of grilled chicken or baked fish, over steamed vegetables, or tossed with hot pasta. You can experiment with these basic combinations in a hundred ways and come up with some great creations! Be sure to label them with a permanent marker, so you don't have to play a flavored-butter guessing game each time you want to use one.

....

LAMB LOIN *with* POMEGRANATE REDUCTION

The flavors of this dish are deep and delish—and, of course, pomegranate is the new miracle food!

1 pound lamb loin

2 teaspoons olive oil

1½ cups pomegranate juice

2 tablespoons red wine vinegar

2 tablespoons butter (optional)

salt and black pepper

pomegranate arils, for garnish

GLUTEN-FREE

Season the lamb loins with salt and black pepper. Heat the oil in a large sauté pan over medium-high heat. Sear the lamb loin well on both sides, about 6 minutes total. Remove to a platter. Pour the pomegranate juice and vinegar into the sauté pan and bring to a boil. Boil until the sauce is thickened and reduced to desired consistency, about 5 minutes. Slice the lamb loin on the bias into ½-inch slices and return the slices to the sauce, along with any accumulated juices. Heat until just cooked through—the lamb should still be pink. Remove the lamb slices to a serving platter. If desired, swirl the butter into the sauce, off the heat. Pour the sauce over the lamb slices to serve. Garnish with pomegranate arils.

Serves: 4

Prep Time: 5 minutes, plus marinating time

Cooking Time: 15 minutes

This would pair beautifully with Cherry Rice Pilaf and steamed green beans.

BURGUNDY LAMB *and* CIPOLLINI

Don't be afraid of lamb. This is a great way to try this flavorful meat—the marinade is delicious and complements the luscious lamb flavor beautifully.

1 tablespoon olive oil

1 pound Trader Joe's Burgundy Pepper Lamb Tips

1 (8-ounce) bag peeled cipollini onions, cut in half

2 cubes frozen crushed garlic

½ cup red wine

½ cup beef broth

GLUTEN-FREE

In a medium sauté pan, heat the olive oil and sauté the lamb cubes over medium-high heat until browned on all sides. Add the onions and sauté 2 minutes. Add garlic and sauté until fragrant. Add red wine, bring to a boil, reduce heat, and simmer 2 to 3 minutes. Add beef broth and simmer 8 to 10 minutes, until lamb and onions are tender and sauce is reduced.

Serves: 4
Prep Time: 5 minutes
Cooking Time: 20 minutes

Chapter 7

PORK

Chops, tenderloins, bacon, speck, pancetta, or prosciutto—I'll just confess up front to being a card-carrying, certified, die-hard porkaholic. When I'm recipe-testing and the dish lacks something, my first thought is what kind of pork to add. A stroll along the Trader Joe's meat aisle will generally offer up several great answers to that question.

If time is tight, I generally reach for pork tenderloins. They're super-affordable, there's no waste, they cook up fast, and there are thousands of ways to change up the flavor. With a simple basting of Trader Joe's Bold and Smoky Kansas City-Style Barbecue Sauce or a maple syrup–mustard glaze, I can turn sliced pork tenderloin into a palate-pleasing dish my family will love. The loin chops go just as quickly from pan to platter with the help of a simple pan sauce or glaze.

While I love pork tenderloins, I hereby proclaim my belief that bacon is a miracle food. The smell of bacon cooking has tempted many a vegetarian off the path. My fondest hope is that bacon, like dark chocolate and red wine, will be declared good for us! While I'm not holding my breath on that one, I do indulge responsibly in the great Niman Ranch Applewood Smoked Dry-Cured Bacon. I think it's the best bacon available in my area, and just a strip or two adds terrific flavor to many dishes. The back of the package tells all about the diet and loving care the pigs are given, which is great—up to a point. Let's not sugar-coat this … in the end, they are bacon. But I do believe animals that are raised in humane conditions, fed well, and given room to move about produce more delicious and healthful meat. So I'm glad Trader Joe's carries this terrific porcine product. After all, one ounce of bacon fat contains less saturated fat and cholesterol than butter. I liberally interpret that to mean that bacon fat is nearly a health food!

So, if meat is on the menu at my house, it's very likely to be the "other white meat," although I personally prefer mine on the pink side. Pork is bred to be so lean these days, it's a shame to overcook it. A very slight blush is a pretty thing, especially when it comes to pork.

GOURMET MAGAZINE-INSPIRED HAM CUPS

The cover of Gourmet *magazine featured these gorgeous presentations in February 2002. Their recipe contained sautéed mushrooms and crème fraîche under the eggs, which is fabulous. Other fillings might include sautéed fennel and goat cheese, caramelized onions and Gouda, or salsa with grated Monterey Jack and cheddar cheese. Use your imagination to create many variations on this simple and eye-catching idea.*

1 tablespoon canola oil

6 slices Niman Ranch Applewood Smoked Cured Black Forest Ham, or other high-quality ham

4 ounces goat cheese

about 9 tablespoons Trader Giotto's Pesto alla Genovese (in the refrigerated section)

6 eggs

GLUTEN-FREE

Preheat oven to 400°F. Lightly oil six ramekins or a muffin tin. Fit a slice of ham into each container, twisting it to form a cup. Put about 1½ tablespoons of pesto in each cup, top with the same amount of cheese, then break an egg on top of each one. Bake until set, about 20 minutes.

Serves: 6
Prep Time: 15 minutes
Cooking Time: 20 minutes

FRAT BRATS

I created this sandwich for my son Kevin when he turned 21. His fraternity brothers come to the cooking school hungry, and these hearty sandwiches can feed a bunch of them in a hurry.

1 package Trader Joe's Hofbrau Brats (bratwurst)

2 red onions, thinly sliced

1 (12-ounce) beer (We used MacTarnahan's Oregon Honey Beer, but you can use whatever you like.)

4 focaccia or panini rolls

about ½ cup Trader Joe's Corn and Chile Tomato-Less Salsa

Garnishes: sliced avocado, sliced Muenster or Havarti cheese, and sliced tomatoes

Place the bratwurst and sliced onions in a medium sauté pan and pour the beer over them. Bring the beer to a boil and simmer the bratwurst 5 minutes. Turn sausages over and continue to cook until beer is nearly evaporated and onions begin to soften and deepen in color, about 10 minutes. Remove onions and set aside. Cook bratwurst until lightly browned on one side, then turn to brown lightly on the other side. Remove from pan and cool slightly. Cut sausages in half lengthwise. (If they are not cooked enough for your liking, return them to the pan, cut side down, for a few minutes to cook them more thoroughly.) Split the focaccia rolls (like hamburger buns) and arrange a bratwurst on the bottom of each roll. Place some of the onions on top of each, and add a dollop of corn salsa. Garnish as desired with avocado, cheese, and tomatoes.

Serves: 4

Prep Time: 5 minutes

Cooking Time: less than 20 minutes

PESTO PORK

This dish is so quick to put together, yet it's flavorful and fancy enough for entertaining.

1 pork tenderloin, sliced into 10 to 12 medallions (rounds) ½-inch-thick

1 tablespoon olive oil

1 (7-ounce) container Trader Giotto's Pesto alla Genovese (in the refrigerated section)

½ cup sherry or dry white wine

salt and pepper

GLUTEN-FREE

Preheat broiler. Lightly season the pork with salt and pepper. In a medium sauté pan, heat the oil and brown half the pork medallions on both sides over medium-high heat, about 5 minutes total. Set aside and repeat with remaining medallions until all pork is cooked. (Leave oil and drippings in the sauté pan.) Spread a dab of pesto on each medallion and place the pork on a baking sheet. Broil until pesto is bubbly, about a minute. Remove pork to a warm platter. Carefully add the sherry to the sauté pan, bring to a boil, reduce heat, and simmer, stirring, until the pan is deglazed and the sauce is syrupy, 2 to 3 minutes. Pour sauce over pork medallions. Serve over brown or white rice or pasta.

Serves: 4
Prep Time: 5 minutes
Cooking Time: 15 minutes

....

For a great tapa, toast some baguette rounds and brush with a little olive oil. Top with a slice of the pork and a drizzle of the tasty sauce.

....

PORK with VERMOUTH

Vermouth is a terrific and underutilized ingredient. If you don't regularly drink wine or don't want to open a bottle just for a recipe, vermouth can stand in. The slightly herbacious flavor will go with many recipes and, once opened, a bottle of vermouth will hold its freshness longer than a bottle of opened wine.

1–1½ pounds pork tenderloin

2 teaspoons butter

3 cubes frozen crushed garlic

½ cup dry vermouth

1 teaspoon fresh rosemary leaves, chopped

½ cup heavy cream

salt and freshly ground pepper

GLUTEN-FREE

Slice the tenderloin into ½-inch-thick medallions and flatten them with the palm of your hand. Season to taste with salt and pepper. In a medium sauté pan, working in batches, sauté in butter over medium heat until browned, about 4 minutes per side. Remove pork to a platter and keep warm. Sauté garlic in the same pan 2 minutes, or until fragrant. Carefully add the vermouth and rosemary and simmer over medium-high heat until reduced by half, about 2 to 3 minutes. Add cream and cook until thickened and slightly reduced. Return pork medallions and accumulated juices to the pan and simmer 2 to 3 minutes, or until cooked through.

Serves: 4
Prep Time: 5 minutes
Cooking Time: 20 minutes

VIGNERON'S SAUSAGES (THE WINEMAKER'S SAUSAGES)

Build a dinner party around this unusual and fun presentation. A green salad, some crusty bread, and some vino, and you're set.

1 pound fresh (not cured) sausages (beef, pork, or chicken)

1 tablespoon butter

2 shallots, thinly sliced

1 cup white Burgundy (or other dry Chardonnay)

2 tablespoons Dijon mustard

1 cup seedless green and/or red grapes

salt and pepper

Preheat oven to 400°F. In a medium sauté pan, cover the sausages with water and simmer 10 minutes. While the sausages poach, dot the butter over the bottom of an ovenproof casserole. Sprinkle the shallots over the butter, and when the sausages have cooked 10 minutes (they will not be completely cooked through), place them on top of the shallots. Pour the wine over the sausages and bake about 35 minutes, turning halfway through the cooking time so that the sausages brown evenly. Remove the sausages and keep warm. Pour the wine-shallot mixture into the sauté pan, bring to a boil, and stir in mustard. Simmer until thickened, about 4 minutes, then add grapes and simmer until just warmed through. Season to taste with salt and pepper, pour sauce over sausages, and serve.

Serves: 4
Prep Time: 5 minutes
Cooking Time: 45 minutes

MAPLE BALSAMIC PORK CHOPS

I'm a big fan of Grade B maple syrup. It's darker in color and, to my palate, deeper in flavor. And it's cheaper than the fancy-schmancy Grade A.

1 tablespoon grapeseed oil

4 Trader Joe's Butcher Shop Natural Boneless Pork Loin Chops

6 tablespoons maple syrup

2 tablespoons balsamic vinegar

1 tablespoon Dijon mustard

Preheat oven to 375°F. In a medium sauté pan, heat the oil and brown the pork chops on both sides over medium-high heat (about 4 minutes per side.) Combine the maple syrup, balsamic vinegar, and mustard, and pour over chops. Place in oven and bake 15 minutes, or until pork is cooked through and light pink in color.

Serves: 4
Prep Time: 5 minutes
Cooking Time: 25 minutes

MARSALA-ROASTED PORK

Here's another main dish that's great for entertaining. The sauce will make you want to lick the plate, so be sure to have something to soak up the delicious liquid.

½ (.88-ounce) package Trader Joe's Mixed Wild Mushroom Medley (You'll find these near the pasta.)

1 (¾ to 1 pound) pork tenderloin

2 teaspoons olive oil

½ cup heavy cream

2 tablespoons Marsala

1 tablespoon Dijon mustard

salt and pepper

Preheat oven to 400°F. In a coffee grinder or food processor, chop the dried mushrooms until they are pulverized. Season the mushroom powder with salt and pepper. Roll the tenderloin in the mushroom powder to coat it evenly. In a sauté pan large enough to hold the tenderloin, heat the olive oil and brown the meat on all sides. Remove the tenderloin to an ovenproof casserole. Combine the cream, Marsala, and mustard, and pour over the tenderloin. Roast until cooked through, about 15 minutes. Let the meat rest at least 5 minutes before slicing.

Serves: 3 to 4
Prep Time: 10 minutes
Cooking Time: 20 minutes

ASIAN-FLAVORED PORK

Quicker than Chinese take-out! If you have leftover cooked rice, or if you use the TJ's frozen rice, this recipe flies together. The scoring of the meat accomplishes two objectives—it creates more surface area for the flavorful spice rub, and it looks so pretty.

4 thin pork loin chops

1 tablespoon salt

1 teaspoon ground cumin

1 teaspoon ground cinnamon

1 teaspoon Trader Joe's Crushed Ginger (in a jar) or minced fresh ginger

2 cubes frozen crushed garlic

2 teaspoons olive oil or grapeseed oil

¼ to ½ cup Trader Joe's General Tsao Stir-Fry Sauce or Sweet Chili Sauce

4 cups cooked white rice

Score the pork chops on both sides, in a diagonal pattern, about ⅛ inch deep. Combine the salt, cumin, cinnamon, crushed ginger, and garlic, and rub on both sides of the pork chops. In a medium sauté pan, heat the oil and sear the pork chops over medium heat on one side, about 3 minutes. Turn and cook on the other side, about 3 minutes. Serve over cooked rice with a splash of General Tsao sauce or Sweet Chili Sauce.

Serves: 4

Prep Time: 10 minutes

Cooking Time: 10 minutes

PORK *and* PEPPERS

A weeknight favorite, this goes together quickly and uses only ¼ cup of wine. You know what to do with the rest ...

2 tablespoons olive oil

1 small onion, sliced thinly

2 cubes frozen crushed garlic

5 to 6 Trader Joe's Minisweet
Bell Peppers, sliced

1 (¾ to 1 pound) pork tenderloin,
cut into ½-inch-thick medallions
(rounds)

¼ cup Sauvignon Blanc or other
dry white wine

1 tablespoon fresh oregano,
chopped, or 1 teaspoon
dried oregano

salt and pepper

GLUTEN-FREE

In a large sauté pan, heat the olive oil, and sauté the onion 3 to 4 minutes over medium-high heat. Add the garlic and peppers, and sauté about 5 minutes more, until peppers are tender. Season the pork lightly with salt and pepper. Add the pork to the sauté pan and cook until browned on all sides, about 5 minutes. Add the wine (and the dried oregano, if using) and simmer about 3 to 4 minutes, until wine is slightly reduced. If using fresh oregano, add at this point. Adjust seasonings to taste with salt and pepper.

Serves: 4
Prep Time: 15 minutes
Cooking Time: 20 minutes

CHERRY PORK *with a* KICK

Hands down, one of our favorites from the cooking school. Fast and packed with flavor.

1 pound pork tenderloin, cut into ¾-inch-thick medallions (rounds)

1 tablespoon olive oil

¾ cup Trader Joe's Cherry Preserves

3 tablespoons crème fraîche

dash of Trader Joe's Chili Pepper Hot Sauce or Jalapeño Pepper Hot Sauce

salt and pepper

GLUTEN-FREE

Season pork with salt and pepper. In a medium sauté pan, heat the oil over medium-high heat and sauté pork medallions, in batches, until they are browned and nearly cooked through, about 6 minutes. Remove to a warm platter. In the same sauté pan, melt the cherry preserves and stir in the crème fraîche. Season to taste with hot sauce, salt, and pepper. Return pork and any accumulated juices to the pan and simmer briefly to marry the flavors.

Serves: 4
Prep Time: 5 minutes
Cooking Time: 15 minutes

PORK *with* CIDER

This dish is so great when the weather turns cool. Add some thick slices of apple or pear if you have some handy. It smells amazing as it simmers!

1 tablespoon olive oil

1½ pound pork tenderloin, cut in bite-sized pieces

1 red onion, cut in eighths

½ teaspoon dried thyme, or leaves from 2 sprigs fresh thyme

1 cup Blackthorn Fermented Cider

1 tablespoon balsamic vinegar

salt and pepper

In a large sauté pan, heat the oil and sauté pork and onion wedges over medium-high heat until browned. Add the thyme, hard cider, and balsamic vinegar, and bring to a boil. Reduce heat, season lightly with salt and pepper, and simmer until pork is cooked and cider is thickened, about 8 minutes. Adjust seasoning to taste.

Serves: 4
Prep Time: 5 minutes
Cooking Time: 15 minutes

Serve something starchy with this, like mashed potatoes or rice, so you can sop up all the sauce!

SPANISH-STYLE PORK

This dish is great on the center of the plate or as a small-plate, tapa-style dish.

2 tablespoons olive oil, divided

1 (¾ to 1 pound) pork tenderloin, cut into ½-inch-thick medallions (rounds)

2 cubes frozen crushed garlic

2 cups sliced mushrooms

½ cup dry sherry

¾ cup orange juice, divided

½ cup sliced green olives stuffed with pimientos (optional)

salt and pepper

GLUTEN-FREE

Season the pork medallions with salt and pepper. Heat 1 tablespoon oil in a medium sauté pan. Brown the pork over medium-high heat on both sides and set aside. Add the rest of the olive oil and sauté the garlic until fragrant, 2 to 3 minutes. Add the mushrooms and sauté until they release their moisture and it evaporates, about 5 minutes. Remove to a platter. Combine sherry with ½ cup of the orange juice and pour into sauté pan. Bring to a boil, reduce heat, and simmer about 3 minutes. Return pork to the pan and simmer 2 to 4 minutes, or until it is cooked through. Remove pork to a serving platter. Add the remaining orange juice and simmer until sauce thickens slightly, about 2 minutes. Stir sliced olives into the mushrooms and put the mixture on the pork. Pour the sauce on top and serve.

Serves: 4
Prep Time: 10 minutes
Cooking Time: 20 minutes

CRANBERRY PORK

I make this as soon as fresh cranberries hit the shelves. It tastes like the season and looks like jewels on the plate.

1 (¾ to 1 pound) pork tenderloin,
1 tablespoon olive oil
1 cup orange juice
1 sprig rosemary
1 cup fresh cranberries
2 tablespoons maple syrup
1 tablespoon balsamic vinegar
salt and pepper

Preheat oven to 400°F. Season pork with salt and pepper. In a medium ovenproof sauté pan, heat the olive oil and brown the tenderloin well on all sides over medium-high heat. Add the orange juice and rosemary sprig and bring to a boil. Add cranberries, maple syrup, and balsamic vinegar, and stir to combine. Place pan in preheated oven and roast about 20 minutes, until pork is cooked through (to an internal temperature of 150°F on a meat thermometer). Remove pork to a cutting board, reserving liquids in the pan, and let it rest at least 5 minutes before slicing. Return pan to cooktop and simmer the liquid until thickened, about 5 minutes. Remove rosemary sprig and serve the sauce over sliced pork.

Serves: 4
Prep Time: 5 minutes
Cooking Time: 30 minutes

I buy bags of cranberries when they're in season and freeze them right in the bags they come in. That way I can make this year-round.

GENERAL TSAO PORK
with RICE STICKS

The General Tsao sauce is on my "desert island" list. Please, Joe, don't ever put this on your dreaded "discontinued" list!

2 teaspoons olive oil

3 cubes frozen crushed garlic

1½ pound pork tenderloin, cut into ½-inch-thick medallions (rounds)

½ cup General Tsao Stir-Fry Sauce

1½ cups chicken broth

handful of haricots verts (French green beans)

½ (13.2-ounce) bag Trader Joe's Rice Sticks (Thai pasta)

½ (10-ounce) bag shredded carrots

In a large sauté pan, heat the oil and sauté the garlic over medium-high heat until aromatic, 1 to 2 minutes. Add the pork and sauté until it begins to brown, 4 to 5 minutes. Add the General Tsao sauce and chicken broth, and bring to a boil. Reduce heat and simmer until pork is cooked, 10 to 12 minutes. While the pork cooks, bring a saucepan of water to a boil and add the green beans and rice sticks. Boil until both are tender, about 5 minutes. Drain the noodles and beans, and toss in the shredded carrots. Top the noodles with the pork and sauce.

Serves: 4
Prep Time: 10 minutes
Cooking Time: 20 minutes

• •
The Rice Sticks can be found with the grains and pad Thai. They're not always available, so stock up when you see them.
• •

MARGARITA PORK CHOPS

The flavor just pops on these babies ... plus, you can use some of the leftover ingredients for some liquid libation!

1 teaspoon ground cumin

4 Trader Joe's Butcher Shop Bone-In Frenched Center-Cut Pork Chops

1 tablespoon olive oil

3 cubes frozen crushed garlic

¼ cup chicken broth

½ cup tequila

2 tablespoons fresh lime juice

4 tablespoons butter

½ jalapeño, minced

salt and freshly ground black pepper

Combine the cumin with 2 teaspoons of salt and about ½ teaspoon freshly ground pepper. Season the pork chops well on both sides with this mixture. (You may have some seasoning mix left over.) In a large sauté pan, heat the oil and brown the chops well, 4 to 5 minutes per side, over medium-high heat. Remove chops to a warmed platter. In the same sauté pan, sauté the garlic until fragrant, 1 to 2 minutes. In a separate bowl, combine the chicken broth, tequila, and lime juice. Remove pan from heat, add liquid, and return to heat. (Have a lid ready to cover the pan in case the alcohol ignites—by combining the liquids, the alcohol has been diluted, but it may flare up). Bring the liquid mixture to a boil and reduce to about ¼ cup. Add the butter and any juices that have accumulated on the platter. Swirl the pan until the butter is incorporated. Season to taste with the minced jalapeño, salt, and pepper. Pour sauce over the chops.

Serves: 4
Prep Time: 10 minutes
Cooking Time: 20 minutes

SPICY APRICOT-GLAZED PORK

The sweet apricot flavor paired with the spicy chili sauce is a big winner. It almost takes longer to preheat the oven than to put this dish together!

4 Trader Joe's Butcher Shop Boneless Pork Loin Chops (about 1 pound)

½ cup Trader Joe's Fresh Apricot Preserves (or orange marmalade)

2 tablespoons Trader Joe's Sweet Chili Sauce

1 tablespoon rice vinegar

salt and pepper

Preheat oven to 400°F. Lightly season pork chops with salt and pepper. Stir together the apricot preserves, Sweet Chili Sauce, and rice vinegar. Brush the pork chops well with the apricot-chili sauce glaze and roast 15 to 20 minutes, or to desired degree of doneness.

Serves: 4
Prep Time: 5 minutes
Cooking Time: 20 minutes

PORK *with* DRIED CRANBERRIES *and* PINE NUTS

When this dish is made with arugula, the vivid greens and reds are just gorgeous. The flavors are vibrant, and the whole thing goes together lickety-split.

⅓ cup dried cranberries

1 cup hot water

⅓ cup olive oil, divided

1½ pound pork tenderloin, cut into ½-inch-thick medallions (rounds)

½ cup pine nuts

4 cloves garlic, minced

3 tablespoons balsamic vinegar

4 ounces arugula or ½ pound cooked pasta

salt and pepper

Soak the dried cranberries in hot water until softened, about 15 minutes. In a medium sauté pan, heat about 1 tablespoon of olive oil over medium-high heat. Working in batches, brown the pork medallions on both sides until just cooked through, about 6 minutes total. Remove cooked pork to a warmed platter. In the same sauté pan, warm the remaining olive oil with the pine nuts just until the nuts begin to smell fragrant and become slightly toasted, about 4 minutes. Add the garlic and cook until golden and fragrant, about 2 minutes. Drain the cranberries and add to the sauté pan, along with the balsamic vinegar. Season to taste with salt and pepper. Arrange pork on top of the arugula or pasta and top with warm sauce.

Serves: 4
Prep Time: 15 minutes
Cooking Time: 20 minutes

Chapter 8

SEAFOOD

I'm really picky about where I buy my fresh fish. Generally, I prefer to buy it from a real, live fishmonger who has kept it on a bed of crushed ice. This helps me assess the freshness of the fish, because one whiff will tell the tale if the filets are less than fresh. While that's not possible at Trader Joe's, I'm willing to bend my rule there for one simple reason: turnover. The fresh fish case is quite small in most TJ's stores, and it's constantly being restocked, so nothing sits there for long. While it is tough to give the fish the sniff test through the plastic wrap, by being vigilant about the packing date, I've had very good luck with the fresh fish purchased at my Joe's. The prices are quite fair, especially when we're talkin' sashimi-grade ahi or wild salmon. The price discount can be big enough that you can pick out a nice bottle of Sauvignon Blanc with your savings. Forget coupons, that's the kind of wallet relief I appreciate!

The frozen fish case at Trader Joe's is replete with choices. Most of the fish there were caught in the wild, not farmed. There has been finger-pointing on both sides of the wild fish vs. farmed fish fray, and while I generally opt for wild fish, I believe the nutritional benefits of fish in your diet are important enough that, for me, farmed fish is better than no fish. In some parts of this country, that's still the only option. The prices are great (duh … it's TJ's), and the variety varies by season. One of my favorite things to stash in my fridge is the Wild Argentine Shrimp. These are meaty morsels with great flavor, and they sauté up in minutes. They're absolutely on my hoarding list because the supply is limited and seasonal. Watch the frozen case for these and stock up for wonderful flavor in shrimp cocktails, stir-fry dishes, or shrimp salads.

If I got a vote with the folks who buy fish for Trader Joe's, I would sure love to see some wild-caught domestic shrimp in that freezer case, because I would love to support the Gulf shrimpers who took such a hit in the Katrina days and are still struggling to recover. Joe, if you're listening, I'd pay a  buck or two more for the privilege of buying that gorgeous shrimp. I bet a lot of other folks would, too. You could make a great case for this in the Fearless Flyer! What better way to support the USA than with a shrimp boil?!

THAI GINGER CARROTS with SHRIMP and GREEN BEANS

The vibrant oranges, greens, and pinks will wow you, and the flavor's even better.

2 tablespoons butter

3 cubes frozen crushed garlic

1 pound raw large shrimp, defrosted, shells and tails removed

1 bag Trader Joe's frozen Thai-Style Soy Ginger Carrots

¼ (16-ounce) bag frozen haricots verts (French green beans)

salt and pepper

In a medium sauté pan, heat the butter, and briefly sauté the garlic. Add the shrimp and sauté over medium-high heat just until they turn pink, 3 to 4 minutes. Remove the shrimp from the pan with tongs or a slotted spoon and set aside. In the same pan, add the Soy Ginger Carrots and green beans to the garlic butter that remains from cooking the shrimp. Sauté 4 to 5 minutes, until vegetables are warmed through and sauce "dots" are melted. Return the shrimp to the pan, and warm through. Adjust seasoning with salt and pepper.

Serves: 4 as a side, 2 as a main course
Prep Time: 5 minutes
Cooking Time: 10 minutes

SHRIMP on POLENTA PILLOWS

Superfast and deeply delicious, this dish makes a great first course, or toss together a green salad to go with it and call it dinner!

1 (18-ounce) roll Trader Joe's Organic Polenta (precooked)

olive oil for brushing or olive oil spray

3 cubes frozen crushed garlic

1 (8.5-ounce) jar Trader Joe's Julienned Sun-Dried Tomatoes, with about 2 tablespoons of the oil removed (see note)

2 tablespoons capers

½ cup dry white wine

1 pound frozen raw large shrimp, thawed and peeled

Preheat broiler. Slice the polenta into ½-inch rounds. Brush or spray with olive oil and place on a baking sheet. Broil, watching carefully, until browned, about 5 minutes. In a medium sauté pan, drizzle 1 tablespoon of the oil from the jar of sun-dried tomatoes and sauté the garlic over medium-high heat until fragrant, about 2 minutes. Add the contents of the jar (sun-dried tomatoes and remaining oil), capers, and white wine. Sauté until the sun-dried tomatoes are softened and heated through. Add the shrimp and sauté until cooked through and coated with sauce, about 5 minutes. Serve over polenta rounds.

Serves: 4 to 6

Prep Time: 5 minutes

Cooking Time: 15 minutes

• •

Use the 2 tablespoons of reserved oil from the jar of sun-dried tomatoes to scramble with eggs or brush on crostini. It's full of flavor from the tomatoes and herbs.

• •

SHRIMP in HARD CIDER

Hard cider is delicious, and really pretty much ignored in the United States. In Europe, it's often served as a tasty alternative to beer, which I really appreciate, since I'm not a big beer fan. The dry, slightly effervescent tang of pear or apple cider brings a crispness to this quick dinner dish.

1 pound raw large shrimp, peeled and deveined

1 tablespoon butter

2 cloves garlic, minced

¼ cup Calvados (or other brandy)

1 cup hard cider (Blackthorn Fermented Cider or Ace pear cider)

salt and pepper

Remove the tail shells from the shrimp, if they are attached. Pat the shrimp dry. In a large sauté pan, heat the butter and sauté the garlic over medium-high heat until fragrant. Add the shrimp and sauté just until pink, 2 to 3 minutes. Remove the shrimp to a platter and carefully add the Calvados (or brandy) to the pan. If it does not ignite, either tip the pan toward the flame (taking care not to spill any of the liquor) or light with a match to burn off the alcohol. Add the cider and bring to a boil. Reduce heat and simmer until liquid is reduced by about half. Return the shrimp to the pan, toss to warm and coat with sauce, and season to taste with salt and pepper.

Serves: 4
Prep Time: 5 minutes
Cooking Time: 10 minutes

ROASTED POTATOES, SHRIMP, and PANCETTA

You'll find the diced prosciutto in the refrigerated case with the cold cuts. This shortcut makes this dish a snap to put together, and it will be gobbled up in about half the time it took to cook it!

2 tablespoons olive oil

1 pound boiling potatoes, cut into small cubes, or 1 pound bag Teeny Tiny Potatoes, left whole

¼ cup diced pancetta

2 cubes frozen crushed garlic

¼ teaspoon red chile pepper flakes

1 pound raw large shrimp, peeled and deveined

¼ cup dry white wine

salt and pepper

2 tablespoons chopped parsley, for garnish

Preheat oven to 450°F. Heat the olive oil in a medium ovenproof sauté pan and sauté the potatoes over medium-high heat until softened and golden, about 10 minutes. Add the pancetta, garlic, red chile pepper flakes, shrimp, and white wine. Season lightly with salt and pepper, and stir to combine. Place the pan into the preheated oven and roast until shrimp are just cooked through, about 10 minutes. Garnish with chopped parsley.

Serves: 4 to 6
Prep Time: 10 minutes
Cooking Time: 25 minutes

GAMBAS y JAMBON

A great addition to a tapas spread. The flavors of shrimp and pork complement each other so well, and the spiciness from the hot sauce sneaks up on you!

1 pound raw large shrimp, peeled and deveined (reserve shells, if you peeled them yourself)

1 tablespoon olive oil

1 tablespoon butter

5 cubes frozen crushed garlic

¼ cup chopped Serrano ham, pancetta, or prosciutto

Trader Joe's Chili Pepper Hot Sauce or Jalapeño Pepper Hot Sauce, to taste

salt and pepper

GLUTEN-FREE

In a sauté pan large enough to hold the shrimp in a single layer, heat the olive oil and butter to bubbling over medium-high heat. If you have the shrimp shells, sauté them until they turn pink and the oil-butter mixture is perfumed with the aroma of shrimp. Remove the shells with tongs or a slotted spoon, shaking the liquid back into the pan. (If no shells are available, begin here.) Add the garlic and sauté until it is fragrant, 2 to 3 minutes. Add the ham, pancetta, or prosciutto and sauté 2 minutes. Add the shrimp and sauté just until pink and opaque, 2 to 4 minutes. Season with salt, pepper, and hot sauce. Serve on baguette toasts as an appetizer or over rice for a main dish.

Serves: 4 as an appetizer, 2 to 3 as a main course
Prep Time: 10 minutes
Cooking Time: 15 minutes

MARGARITA SHRIMP

The margarita theme is a recurring one in these pages—hey, I grew up in Southern California, and margaritas are a summer staple here!

1 tablespoon grapeseed oil

1 medium yellow onion, chopped

3 cubes frozen crushed garlic

1 pound raw large shrimp, peeled and deveined

¼ cup tequila

2 ripe tomatoes, chopped

½ cup shredded carrots

juice of 2 limes

1 ripe avocado, diced

salt and pepper

In a medium sauté pan, heat the oil and sauté the onion over medium-high heat until it begins to soften, 3 to 4 minutes. Add the garlic and sauté until fragrant, 1 to 2 minutes. Add the shrimp and sauté 3 to 4 minutes. Carefully add the tequila, away from the heat. (Or flambé it if you want some drama, but have a lid nearby to quell the flame, if necessary). Add the tomatoes and carrots and sauté 2 minutes. Add the lime juice and cook another minute, or until shrimp is just cooked through. Add the diced avocado, toss to warm through, and season to taste with salt and pepper.

Serves: 4 as an appetizer, 2 to 3 as a main course

Prep Time: 10 minutes

Cooking Time: 15 minutes

SWEET-GLAZED SALMON with CORN SALSA

The spiciness of the corn salsa pairs so well with the rich salmon. If you haven't figured it out yet, the Corn and Chile Tomato-Less Salsa is one of my all-time favorite TJ's products. It just looks like a party in the jar, and it goes on nearly everything.

3 tablespoons Organic Blue Agave Sweetener

1 tablespoon Trader Joe's Crushed Ginger (in a jar) or minced fresh ginger

2 cubes frozen crushed garlic

1 tablespoon rice vinegar

1 pound salmon filets, fresh or, if frozen, defrosted

about ½ cup Trader Joe's Corn and Chile Tomato-Less Salsa

Preheat oven to 425°F. Stir together the agave syrup, ginger, garlic, and vinegar. Place the salmon in an ovenproof casserole and brush with the glaze. Roast until fish is just barely cooked through, 8 to 10 minutes. Remove from oven and top with corn salsa.

Serves: 4
Prep Time: 5 minutes
Cooking Time: less than 15 minutes

GLAMOUR SALMON

I hate to think of how long ago I saw a version of this recipe in Glamour *magazine. Let's just say I was a new bride—and it was in another century. I was so proud of myself when I served this to guests at a dinner party because it was elegant and tasty. That hasn't changed over the ensuing decades.*

1 to 1½ pounds salmon filets

⅓ cup honey

2 tablespoons soy sauce

juice of 1 lemon

1 tablespoon sesame oil

¼ teaspoon red chile pepper flakes

salt and pepper, to taste

Place filets in a resealable plastic bag. Combine remaining ingredients and pour over fish. Preheat broiler and broiler pan while fish marinates, about 20 minutes. Place filets, skin side down, on broiler pan, and place in the oven at least 4 inches from the heating element. Broil 5 to 7 minutes, until nearly opaque.

Serves: 4 to 6

Prep Time: 25 minutes (mostly marinating time)

Cooking Time: less than 10 minutes

SOUTH of FRANCE HALIBUT

When I imagine lazy summer days in Arles or Avignon, I don't envision hours of prep work for delicious meals. This dish goes together in the time it takes to sip one glass of rosé.

1 (13.4-ounce) jar Trader Joe's Ratatouille

2 cubes frozen crushed garlic

½ cup dry white wine

1 pound wild halibut, frozen or defrosted

salt, pepper, and red chile pepper flakes

In a medium sauté pan, combine the ratatouille, garlic, and white wine and bring to a simmer. Add the fish and simmer until it is cooked through (about 6 minutes for thawed fish, and about 20 minutes for frozen). Season to taste with salt, pepper, and red chile pepper flakes.

Serves: 4

Prep Time: 5 minutes

Cooking Time: less than 10 minutes for thawed fish, and about 20 minutes for frozen

Chapter 9

PASTA

onestly, who isn't immediately comforted by a softly steamy, fragrant, cheese-stringed, yielding bowl of pasta? A day has to be nearly disastrous before the thought of that very meal won't lift my spirits. The pasta aisle may be my favorite one at Trader Joe's, and pasta is definitely my favorite dinner for a harried night. I think most of us turn to pasta when hunger is high and time or energy is in short supply. Pasta is a great way to tart up leftovers so no one will recognize (and thereby complain about) them.

If I am so distracted or overtired that thinking about what to cook is overwhelming, I find that if I get the pasta water going and salted and just let myself sway around the kitchen, pasta-making ingredients will almost magically bring themselves to my fingertips, like the brooms in the Sorcerer's Apprentice. Last night was one of those nights. (Hey! cookbook writing is *hard!*) So I poured a glass of Sauvignon Blanc, got the salted water boiling, grabbed a bag of farfalle, and tossed some in. I had a shallot, so I chopped that up, then poured a glug of good TJ's olive oil in a sauté pan. Once the shallot smelled great, I noticed that I had a hank of asparagus hanging around, so I whacked the spears into pieces and threw them in to relax. There was a handful of mushrooms, so in it went, and by then the pasta was nearly tender. I sloshed about a cupful of pasta water into a cup for later and drained off the rest. A glug of cream and a knob of goat cheese went into the pan of vegetables and immediately surrendered into creamy sauce. I literally ripped the remaining meat off a rotisserie chicken from the fridge and tossed the chunks in to warm up. I squeezed the contents of a tube of chicken broth concentrate on top and splashed in the pasta water I'd saved. A quick stir, and I dumped the cooked noodles into the pan. A couple grinds of black pepper from the great TJ's plastic pepper grinder, and dinner had practically cooked itself. All I did was stroll around my kitchen with a glass of wine for 15 minutes (and create this bonus recipe for you!)

Pasta shapes are so varied, and the different varieties are fun to pair with so many flavor profiles. The sharp flavors of olives and lemons, the peppery notes of arugula or radicchio, the smooth creaminess of mascarpone or crème fraîche, the crunch of nuts or toasted bread crumbs? Any of these combine beautifully (and quickly) with Trader Joe's pastas for a fast, satisfying carb-lover's bowlful of love. A gigantic pot of well-salted water is the key. "Salty like the sea," I always recall my culinary school instructor bellowing. You want enough water for that pasta to be able to swish around like clothes in the washing machine. Too little water makes for stuck-together clumps of noodles. Use the package instructions as a guide on timing, but trust yourself more than those—fish out a strand when it looks pliable and take a nibble. The texture should be the slightest bit firm at the center, but sans crunch. The pasta will continue to cook a little bit as you drain it and as it rests in the strainer, so you want a little resistance to the tooth before you do that. But no crunch—"al dente" means "to the tooth," not "break a tooth"!

We all need to let our inner carb fiend out to play every now and again. Gluten-free, whole wheat, or traditional, fresh or dried, Joe's has a pasta that will have you setting a pot of water to boil and reaching for the colander. (Oh, and opening the wine. Don't forget that important step!) Many of these dishes are a meal in a bowl on their own, but pairing them with a great salad is never a bad idea.

OLIVE BUTTERFLIES

I love to serve this in summer as an accompaniment to grilled meat or fish. The tapenade delivers a tangy saltiness, and the goat cheese melts into a lightly creamy sauce.

1 (16-ounce) bag farfalle

1 (10-ounce) jar green Olive Tapenade (or Roasted Red Pepper and Artichoke Tapenade)

4 ounces goat cheese (Trader Joe's Chèvre, Silver Goat Chèvre, or Madame Chèvre)

handful of cherry tomatoes, halved (optional)

salt and pepper

VEGETARIAN

Cook the pasta in boiling, salted water until tender. Drain and return to the saucepan with the tapenade and goat cheese, stirring to incorporate and melt the cheese. Stir in tomatoes, if using. Adjust seasoning to taste with salt and pepper.

Serves: 4

Prep Time: 5 minutes, if using halved tomatoes

Cooking Time: 10 minutes

We sometimes call these *bowties*, but the Italians call them *farfalle*, which means butterflies. Much more poetic than bowties, don't ya think? This is great hot, served at room temperature, or chilled.

PASTA MOLLICA

Mollica *means crumb in Italian, but in this dish, it also means delicious! Students at the cooking school always look skeptical before they taste the deeply nutty, crunchy flavor these little nuggets bring to the pasta. It's an old technique: when times were tough, people learned to use up everything and to substitute the browned crumbs of leftover bread for more expensive nuts or even for cheese. In the current economy,* mollica *may become a household term again.*

1 (16-ounce) bag long pasta (such as linguine or spaghetti), cooked al dente and drained

4 tablespoons butter or olive oil, divided

2 cubes frozen crushed garlic

½ cup fresh bread crumbs (don't use dry bread crumbs from the package for this)

salt and pepper

VEGETARIAN, VEGAN *(if olive oil and vegan bread are used)*

Melt 2 tablespoons of the butter in a medium sauté pan (or use 2 tablespoons of oil) and sauté the garlic over medium heat for 1 to 2 minutes, or just until fragrant. Add the bread crumbs and sauté until browned and crispy, about 5 minutes. (The crumbs should be very nicely colored and crisp, but be careful not to burn them.) Toss the cooked pasta with the reserved butter or olive oil, and then with the bread crumbs. Season to taste with salt and pepper.

Serves: 4
Prep Time: 5 minutes
Cooking Time: 10 minutes

• •
To make fresh bread crumbs, finely chop some good bread in a food processor. I like to use the Trader Joe's Artisan-style Whole Grain Loaf for this, but a good baguette will work well, too.
• •

FARFALLE *with* GREEN BEANS *and* FETA

I love the flirty look of farfalle. The green beans add nutrition to this dish, of course, but they also look so pretty, and the crumbled feta gets sprinkled in like confetti.

1 (16-ounce) bag farfalle

1 cup fresh green beans, cut into 3-inch pieces or 1 cup fresh haricots verts (French green beans) or frozen French green beans, whole

3 ounces feta cheese

salt and pepper

½ pound cooked medium shrimp (optional)

1 tablespoon butter (optional)

VEGETARIAN
(if made without shrimp)

Bring a large pot of salted water to a boil. Add the pasta and cook until nearly al dente. (The pasta should be cooked about three-quarters of the way through.) Add the green beans and continue to cook until beans are tender, 3 to 5 minutes. Drain the pasta and beans and place in a serving dish. Toss in the feta, crumbling as you add it, and stir to combine. Taste the pasta before you season it because the feta is salty—you may only need some freshly ground black pepper.

Serves: 4
Prep Time: 5 minutes
Cooking Time: 15 minutes

....

Adding ½ pound of cooked large shrimp to this makes it a meal in a bowl. Just sauté the shrimp for 2 to 3 minutes in 1 tablespoon of butter over medium-high heat to warm through, and then toss with the pasta.

....

LEMON-VODKA PASTA

These simple but classic flavor combinations never disappoint. I guess that's why they're classics! This goes really well with roasted chicken or fish.

1 (16-ounce) bag long, thin pasta (linguini, spaghetti, or capellini)

1 (8-ounce) container mascarpone

zest and juice of 1 lemon

2 tablespoons vodka (or limoncello)

½ cup fresh basil leaves, chiffonaded

salt and pepper

VEGETARIAN

Bring a large pot of salted water to a boil. Cook the pasta al dente. While the pasta cooks, in a medium saucepan, warm the mascarpone with the lemon juice and vodka. Season to taste with salt and pepper. When the pasta is cooked, drain it and toss it with the fresh basil and lemon zest. Add the pasta to the sauce in the pan and toss to coat. Adjust seasonings to taste with salt and pepper and serve.

Serves: 4

Prep Time: 5 minutes

Cooking Time: 10 minutes

. . . .

When you need the zest and juice of a lemon, always zest first and juice second. It's *so* much easier to get the zest off of the intact lemon instead of trying to zest the two halves.

. . . .

PASTA with PUMPKIN SAUCE

The Trader Joe's canned pumpkin is organic and is really great quality. I don't even want to tell you how many cans of it I squirrel away when it arrives in the stores. Since it's a seasonal item, I need to make sure I have enough to last the year.

1 (16-ounce) bag pasta (see note)

1 cup Trader Joe's canned Organic Pumpkin Purée

1 cup chicken broth

splash of Trader Joe's Chili Pepper Hot Sauce or Jalapeño Pepper Hot Sauce, or sprinkling of red chile pepper flakes

salt and pepper

½ cup toasted walnuts, coarsely chopped

2 teaspoons fresh sage, finely minced

shaved Parmesan cheese (optional)

Bring a large pot of salted water to a boil. Cook the pasta al dente. Reserve about a cup of the cooking water before draining the pasta and placing it in a large bowl. In a small saucepan, combine the pumpkin purée and chicken broth and bring to a simmer. Pour over the cooked pasta, adding the reserved cooking liquid, ¼ cup at a time, until the sauce reaches the desired consistency. Toss to combine and season to taste with a little hot sauce or red chile pepper flakes, salt, and pepper. Add the chopped walnuts and minced sage and toss again. Garnish with shaved Parmesan, if using.

Serves: 4
Prep Time: 5 minutes
Cooking Time: 15 minutes

• •
Long or short shapes of pasta work equally well in this dish, so use whatever you have on hand.
• •

LINGUINI with LEEKS, SHRIMP, and ARUGULA

I'm a sucker for the pink-and-green look of this dish. The leeks, arugula, and shrimp get all tangled up in the long pasta strands, and the grated Parmesan provides a nutty saltiness I just love.

1 (16-ounce) bag linguini (or another long pasta), cooked and drained

1 tablespoon olive oil

1 tablespoon butter

2 leeks, cleaned and thinly sliced

2 cubes frozen crushed garlic

½ cup vegetable broth

½ pound medium shrimp, peeled and deveined

a handful of arugula

¼ cup freshly grated Parmesan cheese

salt and pepper

In a medium sauté pan, heat the olive oil and butter. Sauté the leeks over medium-high heat until tender, about 5 minutes. Add the garlic and sauté 1 to 2 minutes, until fragrant. Add the vegetable broth and bring to a boil. Reduce heat and simmer 5 minutes, until the sauce is slightly reduced. Add the shrimp and cook 3 to 4 minutes, until pink. Toss the leek-shrimp mixture with the cooked pasta. Add the arugula and toss. Add the grated Parmesan, toss, and adjust seasonings to taste with salt and pepper.

Serves: 4
Prep Time: 5 minutes
Cooking Time: 25 minutes

PASTA PROVENÇAL

Serving this for lunch is the quickest route to an imaginary afternoon in Avignon. Pair it with a glass of rosé and you may never want to come back home.

1 (16-ounce) bag linguine or another long pasta shape

½ cup shredded carrots

1 tablespoon Trader Joe's Capers in Vinegar, rinsed

½ cup pitted, mixed olives, coarsely chopped

1 (6-ounce) can Skipjack Tuna in Water (or another high-quality tuna)

1 tablespoon olive oil

salt and pepper

Bring a large pot of salted water to a boil. Cook the pasta al dente. Place the carrots in a strainer and pour the pasta in to drain. (The boiling water will blanch the carrots perfectly.) Place the pasta and carrots in a large serving bowl and toss with capers, chopped olives, and tuna. Dress to taste with olive oil, salt, and pepper.

Serves: 4
Prep Time: 5 minutes
Cooking Time: 10 minutes

You can substitute half a jar of green Olive Tapenade for the chopped olives, if you are in a hurry.

GORGONZOLA FUSILLI

It just sounds wonderful, doesn't it? Gor-gon-zola Fu-si-lli ... almost like an Italian mantra. With the optional addition of pancetta or bacon, I just might make it my own mantra!

1 (16-ounce) bag fusilli

2 tablespoons butter

1 shallot, minced

1 leek, thinly sliced

2 tablespoons heavy cream

3 ounces crumbled Gorgonzola cheese

freshly ground black pepper

about 3 ounces diced pancetta or cooked and crumbled Niman Ranch Applewood Smoked Dry-Cured Bacon (optional)

VEGETARIAN *(if no pancetta or bacon is used)*

Bring a large pot of salted water to a boil. Cook the pasta al dente and reserve about a cup of the cooking water before draining the pasta and setting it aside. In the same pot, melt the butter, then sauté the shallot and leek slices over medium heat until slightly caramelized, about 5 minutes. Add the cream, warm through, and add the crumbled Gorgonzola. Allow the cheese to soften. Add the cooked pasta back into the pot and toss to combine. If a more liquid consistency is desired, add a little of the reserved pasta water. Season with freshly ground black pepper. Toss in the pancetta or cooked bacon, if using.

Serves: 4
Prep Time: 5 minutes
Cooking Time: 15 minutes

ONE-POT PESTO PASTA, POTATOES, and GREEN BEANS

The first time I heard of this classic Ligurian dish, I thought it sounded so strange. Talk about carb overload! But the flavors, textures, and colors couldn't be more perfectly paired, and you'll be converted to the pasta-and-potato combination with the first bite.

1 large boiling potato (or two small ones)

½ pound green beans, trimmed and cut into 3-inch lengths

½ (16-ounce) bag thin pasta, such as capellini or spaghetti

½ cup Trader Giotto's Pesto alla Genovese (in the refrigerated section)

2 ounces soft goat cheese (Trader Joe's Chèvre, Silver Goat Chèvre, or Madame Chèvre)

salt and pepper

VEGETARIAN

Bring a large pot of salted water to a boil. Meanwhile, scrub the potato and cut into 1-inch cubes. Place the potato cubes in the boiling water and cook until barely tender, about 7 minutes. Scoop the potatoes out of the water with a slotted spoon and set aside. Add the green beans to the same water and cook until just tender, 5 to 6 minutes. Remove with a slotted spoon and add to the potatoes. In the same water, cook the pasta until tender. When you drain the pasta, reserve ½ cup of the cooking water. In the pasta pot, combine the pesto, goat cheese, and ¼ cup of the water, then add the cooked pasta and toss. Add the potatoes and green beans. If a saucier consistency is desired, add a bit more of the reserved pasta water. Adjust seasonings to taste with salt and pepper.

Serves: 2
Prep Time: 5 minutes
Cooking Time: 30 minutes

• •
Leftovers of this dish are excellent as a cold salad the next day.
• •

A MEAL ON ITS OWN PASTA

The Chard of Many Colors looks like it spilled out of a crayon box, and it couldn't be better for you. The goat cheese adds a creamy element, and it's so subtle in this dish, even people who aren't fans of goat cheese will gobble this up.

1 (16-ounce) bag fusilli or farfalle

6 strips Niman Ranch Applewood Smoked Dry-Cured Bacon, snipped or chopped

2 shallots, thinly sliced

1 tablespoon olive oil

½ bag (about 3 cups) Trader Joe's Chard of Many Colors, coarsely chopped

2 cubes frozen crushed garlic

4 ounces soft goat cheese (Trader Joe's Chèvre, Silver Goat Chèvre, or Madame Chèvre)

salt and freshly ground black pepper

Bring a large pot of salted water to a boil. Cook the pasta al dente. Reserve about a cup of the cooking water before draining the pasta and setting it aside. Once the pasta is drained, in the same pot, cook the bacon until the fat is rendered and the bacon is about half-cooked. Add the shallots and sauté over medium heat until tender and fragrant, 2 to 3 minutes. Add the olive oil and the chard. Sauté until the chard wilts. If it seems too dry, add a few tablespoons of the reserved pasta water. Add the garlic and sauté until it is aromatic, 1 to 2 minutes. In a large bowl, add the chard mixture to the pasta and toss to combine. In the same pot, heat the goat cheese with ½ cup pasta water until it is creamy, then toss with the pasta. Use the remaining pasta water if you want a saucier consistency. Season to taste with freshly ground black pepper and a little salt, if needed.

Serves: 4
Prep Time: 10 minutes
Cooking Time: 20 minutes

••
The bacon and goat cheese will add saltiness, so taste before you add salt.
••

LOTSA LEMON PASTA

I like to think that the healthy arugula balances out the crème fraîche ... Whatever—a little bit of this tasty pasta is all I need to feel satisfied.

1 (7-ounce) bag arugula

1 (7.5-ounce) container crème fraîche

juice and zest of 2 lemons, divided

1 cup grated Parmesan cheese, divided

1 (16-ounce) bag fusilli (or other small pasta)

freshly ground black pepper

VEGETARIAN

Roughly chop the arugula and place in a colander. In a large bowl, stir together the crème fraîche, lemon juice, half the lemon zest, and half the Parmesan cheese. Bring a large pot of salted water to a boil and cook the pasta al dente. Drain the pasta into the colander with the arugula. (The hot water will wilt the arugula slightly.) In the large bowl, toss the pasta with the crème fraîche sauce and season to taste with freshly ground black pepper. Garnish with the remaining grated cheese.

Serves: 4 to 6
Prep Time: 10 minutes
Cooking Time: 15 minutes

BBQ PASTA SALAD

I raise my right hand and proclaim that I am not *a pasta salad fan, but this one has me rethinking that statement. I love the zing of barbecue sauce in this, and the corn salsa wakes the pasta right up. If there's a more colorful pasta salad out there, I've yet to see it. Sign up to bring (yawn) the pasta salad to a potluck, and wow them with this one.*

1 (16-ounce) bag farfalle or penne

½ cup plain yogurt (regular or nonfat)

¼ cup crème fraîche

½ cup Trader Joe's All Natural Barbecue Sauce or TJ's Bold and Smoky Kansas City-Style Barbecue Sauce

2 tablespoons red wine vinegar

1 cup Trader Joe's Corn and Chile Tomato-Less Salsa

4 Trader Joe's Minisweet Peppers, chopped

1 cup Trader Joe's Mixed Medley Cherry Tomatoes, some sliced in half

salt and pepper

3 green onions, chopped

VEGETARIAN

Cook the pasta in a large pot of rapidly boiling salted water until al dente. Drain and rinse under cold running water. In a large bowl, combine the yogurt, crème fraîche, barbecue sauce, and vinegar. Toss the pasta with this mixture, and then add the salsa, chopped peppers, and tomatoes. Season to taste with salt and pepper and garnish with chopped green onions.

Serves: 4 to 6

Prep Time: 10 minutes

Cooking Time: 10 minutes

• •

The only time I ever rinse cooked pasta is when I'm using it for pasta salad. For hot pasta dishes, drain, but skip the rinsing step so the starch will help the sauce adhere to the hot pasta. Rinsing for cold pastas stops the cooking process, which will keep the pasta from getting mushy and will help the pasta soak up the dressing.

• •

BEST PASTA KEVIN EVER HAD

After high school, my son Kevin set off on a wonderful European trip. He visited a lot of places his poor ol' mom had never visited, which I gently reminded him of on every phone call: "Where are you today? Barcelona? Is it great? I've never been …" His travels included many wonderful food adventures, but thankfully, when he returned, he was hungry for my cooking. This was a big hit in his first days back home.

1 (16-ounce) bag penne

3 strips bacon, cut into strips

1 (12.8-ounce) package Trader Joe's Smoked Andouille Chicken Sausage, sliced in ½-inch rounds

1 cup greens (chard, collard, or mustard), coarsely chopped

pinch red chile pepper flakes

salt and pepper

½ cup vermouth

½ cup heavy cream

½ cup Trader Joe's Burrata or Ricotta cheese (optional)

Bring a large pot of salted water to a boil and cook the pasta al dente, then drain, reserving ½ cup of the pasta water, and set the pasta aside. In a sauté pan, sauté the bacon over medium-high heat until nearly crisp, then add the sausage and warm through. Add the greens and red chile pepper flakes and sauté until softened, about 5 minutes. Season to taste with salt and pepper. Remove this mixture to a plate. Reduce heat, add the vermouth to the pan and simmer about 3 minutes, until syrupy. Add cream and simmer about 2 minutes, until thickened slightly. Toss the pasta in the sauce (add a bit of pasta water if needed to thin the sauce). Place the pasta on individual plates or on a platter. Top with a dollop of ricotta or burrata, if using, and then with the bacon-sausage-greens mixture.

Serves: 4
Prep Time: 10 minutes
Cooking Time: 30 minutes

••

I like to describe burrata as a water balloon of mozzarella. A thin layer of mozzarella encases an amazing combination of mozzarella and thickened cream. It's quite perishable, so use it within a day or two of purchase.

••

RED WINE PASTA

I first ate this at a crazy little trattoria in Florence, where they throw you out of the place if you order your steak well-done. While I would never *do that, just to be safe, I stuck to the wine-y pasta and was so happy I did!*

1 (16-ounce) bag spaghetti, capellini, or other long pasta

1 bottle red wine

4 cubes frozen crushed garlic

red chile pepper flakes

2 tablespoons butter

salt and pepper

½ (8-ounce) container crumbled Gorgonzola

½ cup toasted walnuts

VEGETARIAN

Bring a large pot of salted water to a boil and cook the pasta for about 3 minutes, until just pliable. Drain the pasta. In a large sauté pan, bring about three-quarters of the wine to a boil. Add the garlic cubes and a few shakes of red chile pepper flakes. When the garlic has dissolved, add the pasta and cook, stirring frequently, until pasta is al dente. Stir in the butter and season to taste with salt and pepper. Serve individual portions (or put the spaghetti on a platter) and garnish with crumbled Gorgonzola and toasted walnuts.

Serves: 4

Prep Time: 5 minutes

Cooking Time: 20 minutes

• •

I like the Trader Giotto's Organic Spaghetti and a bottle of Old Moon Zinfandel for this. An inexpensive but drinkable Zinfandel or Syrah is a perfect choice for this unusual cooking method.

• •

FETTUCCINE *with* SHRIMP *and* SAFFRON CRÈME

Saffron is the most expensive spice on the planet because it is incredibly labor-intensive to harvest. But Trader Joe's carries an excellent-quality saffron in an adorable cork-topped jar for a great price.

1 (16-ounce) bag fettuccine

1 tablespoon olive oil

1 tablespoon butter

3 cubes frozen crushed garlic

generous pinch of Trader Joe's Spanish Saffron, crumbled

1 cup dry white wine

1 pound raw large shrimp, peeled and deveined (or ½ pound shrimp and ½ pound scallops)

½ cup crème fraîche

salt and pepper

pinch of red chile pepper flakes (optional)

zest of 1 lemon, for garnish

Cook the pasta in rapidly boiling salted water until al dente. Reserve about a cup of the cooking liquid before draining and setting aside. In a medium sauté pan, heat the olive oil and butter over medium heat. Add the garlic and saffron and sauté over medium heat until fragrant, about 2 minutes. Add the wine, bring to a boil, reduce heat and simmer until reduced, about 4 minutes. Add the shrimp and sauté until just cooked through, about 4 minutes. Stir in the crème fraîche and season to taste with salt, pepper, and red chile pepper flakes (if using). Toss with cooked pasta, adding some of the cooking liquid if desired for a saucier consistency. Garnish with lemon zest.

Serves: 4

Prep Time: 10 minutes

Cooking Time: 15 minutes

Chapter 10

VEGETABLES

Whether fresh or frozen, the array of vegetables at Trader Joe's will get you eating your greens … and your oranges, reds, yellows, and browns. Isn't that what the dieticians say? "Eat the rainbow." TJ's makes it easy and tasty to follow that advice. The bags of cleaned and sliced mushrooms are so handy for quick sautés, pasta sauces, or salads, and the shredded carrots are a shortcut I take nearly every week. Sure, I know I'm paying more for the convenience factor, but they save me so much precious time that I'm willing to scrimp elsewhere. Also, my knife skills are decent, but it would take me eons to get all those perfect little slivers out of a bunch of whole carrots! I love to sneak those into a tomato sauce to balance out the acidity. Of course, they're great in a salad, or a wrap, or pasta … you'll find a ton of uses for those little slivers of sweet, colorful crunch.

The fresh vegetable area is full of ingredients that are prepped for your quick cooking pleasure, from the pre-trimmed French green beans called haricots verts to the cut-up cauliflower, to the pre-chopped mirepoix (for really crazy days). As for me, most days I actually enjoy the rhythm of my knife gliding through the carrots, onions, and celery as I get my vegetables ready for whatever's on tap. But at certain crunch times, knowing that the prepped vegetables are waiting can really mean the difference between home cooking and take-out. And I'm always in favor of home cooking, even if it means some corner-cutting.

For purists, Trader Joe has shelves stocked with potatoes and onions of every hue, as well as a glorious palette of peppers. I especially love the Minisweet Bell Peppers. I call them the "weeknight pepper," because when time is tight, these little gems really come through. They have few, if any, seeds, and since that cottony membrane that's sometimes found in larger bell peppers isn't present in the little guys, chopping them takes mere seconds. I cut crosswise, starting at the tip and working toward the stem end, stopping just shy of the top, where a few little seeds may lurk. I enjoy the look of the little "Olympic rings" that result from this technique, but if a more minced texture is needed, it only takes a few seconds to run a knife through the circles of pepper to achieve a nicely chopped pile o' peppers. These sweet little beauties are also terrific cut in half lengthwise and used as a scoop for hummus or another tasty dip.

The vegetable freezer case is full of inspiration, too, whether it's the terrific French green beans or the roasted corn, complete with smoky charred flavor. The vegetable blends can perk up a dinner plate with great color, texture, and flavor. So whether fresh or frozen is your preference, Trader Joe's has a great selection of vegetables to get you eating what's good for you.

GREEN BEANS *with* RED ONION *and* CREAMY FETA DRESSING

This dish is great as is, or you can toss in some leftover steamed or roasted new potatoes for a heartier version.

1 (16-ounce) package fresh green beans, trimmed and steamed

½ red onion, thinly sliced

DRESSING:

½ cup plain yogurt

¾ cup feta cheese, crumbled

1 tablespoon lemon juice or red wine vinegar

freshly ground black pepper

2 tablespoons chopped basil, for garnish

VEGETARIAN

Arrange green beans on a serving plate and scatter most of the red onion slices over the surface, reserving a few. Whisk together the dressing ingredients. (The dressing will be thick, with pieces of feta throughout.) Dollop the dressing over the salad and garnish with reserved red onion slices and basil.

Serves: 4 to 6

Prep Time: 10 minutes

Cooking Time: 10 minutes

. . . .

The frozen French green beans would work for this recipe, too—defrosted, of course!

. . . .

GREEN BEANS with CAMBOZOLA SAUCE

This sauce is so rich and luscious, I could just drink it— but the green beans make this a much healthier idea.

1 package green beans, trimmed (or asparagus, or a combination of both)

4 tablespoons heavy cream or crème fraîche

6 ounces Cambozola or other soft blue cheese

VEGETARIAN, POSSIBLY GLUTEN-FREE *(check Cambozola label)*

Cook the green beans in rapidly boiling, salted water until crisp-tender, 6 to 8 minutes. Drain and refresh in cold water. In a medium saucepan, heat the cream over low heat and melt the cheese. Add the green beans and toss to coat. Adjust seasonings to taste with salt and pepper.

Serves: 4
Prep Time: 5 minutes
Cooking Time: 10 minutes

ROASTED ZUCCHINI and MUSHROOMS with PESTO

These smell amazing while they're roasting, and they look as good as they taste. Throw in some red onion, if there's some handy.

1 pound (about 4 medium) zucchini

1 (8-ounce) container crimini mushrooms

½ red onion, sliced (optional)

1 tablespoon olive oil

1 (8-ounce) container Trader Giotto's Pesto alla Genovese (in the refrigerated section), divided

1 (4-ounce) container Trader Joe's Crumbled Goat Cheese

VEGETARIAN, GLUTEN-FREE

Preheat oven to 425°F. Cut the zucchini into about 1-inch rounds. Toss the zucchini, mushrooms, and red onion (if using) with olive oil and arrange on a baking sheet. Roast until tender, 15 to 20 minutes. Remove vegetables to a serving dish, toss with about half of the pesto, and sprinkle with crumbled goat cheese. Serve with the remaining pesto on the side.

Serves: 4 to 6
Prep Time: 5 minutes
Cooking Time: 20 minutes

SAUTÉED CHARD of MANY COLORS with PINE NUTS

The colors are gorgeous, and the chard is so good for you. This is a great side dish for roast meats, or served on top of pasta.

1 (16-ounce) bag Trader Joe's Chard of Many Colors, coarsely chopped

1 cup chicken or vegetable broth, or water

juice of ½ lemon

2 tablespoons olive oil

2 tablespoons pine nuts, toasted

salt and pepper

pinch of red chile pepper flakes

VEGETARIAN *(if made with water or vegetable broth)*, GLUTEN-FREE

In a large sauté pan over medium heat, cook the chard with the broth or water and lemon juice until tender, about 8 minutes. Drain the liquid, add the olive oil, and sauté the chard over medium-high heat for 3 to 4 minutes. Toss in the pine nuts and season with salt, pepper, and red chile pepper flakes.

Serves: 4 to 6
Prep Time: 5 minutes
Cooking Time: 15 minutes

ROASTED ASPARAGUS *with* HAZELNUTS *and* CLEMENTINES

Close your eyes and picture how great this looks on the plate. Or check out the photo, if your imagination is taking the day off. Just makes you want to dive in with your fingers, doesn't it?

1 (12-ounce) package fresh asparagus

drizzle of olive oil

handful of chopped hazelnuts

2 clementines, peeled and sliced (not sectioned)

salt and freshly ground black pepper

shaved Parmesan cheese, for garnish

VEGETARIAN, GLUTEN-FREE

Preheat oven to 450°F. Place the asparagus on a rimmed baking sheet and drizzle with a little olive oil. Roast 5 minutes. Scatter hazelnuts on top of the asparagus and roast another 3 to 4 minutes. Place on a serving plate and scatter clementine slices on top. Season with a little salt and freshly ground black pepper and garnish with shaved Parmesan cheese.

Serves: 2 to 4
Prep Time: 5 minutes
Cooking Time: 10 minutes

SUGAR SNAP PEAS, CORN, and BACON with BASIL BUTTER

The basil butter is also great on freshly roasted or steamed ears of corn, or even on a steak or pasta.

BASIL BUTTER:

½ cup firmly packed basil leaves

1 cube frozen crushed garlic

½ cup butter

zest of 1 lemon and juice of half

salt and pepper

4 strips Niman Ranch Applewood Smoked Dry-Cured Bacon, chopped

1 (12-ounce) package fresh Trader Joe's Sugar Snap Peas

½ cup Trader Joe's Corn and Chile Tomato-Less Salsa

GLUTEN-FREE

FOR BASIL BUTTER: Place the basil leaves in a food processor and chop finely. Add the garlic cube and butter, and process to combine. Add the lemon juice and zest, and process again. Season to taste with salt and pepper. Wrap in parchment paper or plastic wrap and chill until ready to use.

In a medium sauté pan, cook the bacon until almost crisp. Add the sugar snap peas and sauté over medium-high heat 3 to 4 minutes, until tender. Remove from the pan with a slotted spoon, leaving excess bacon drippings behind. In a serving bowl, toss the peas and bacon with the corn salsa. Top with a tablespoon or two of basil butter and stir to melt the butter. Refrigerate or freeze the rest for another use.

Serves: 2 to 4
Prep Time: 5 minutes
Cooking Time: 10 minutes

ROASTED BUTTERNUT SQUASH with PECANS, DRIED CHERRIES, and BLUE CHEESE

The flavors in this dish could not be more autumnal (a word I truly love). The sage adds an earthy undertone, the colors mimic those of fallen leaves, and the blue cheese brings such depth of flavor. I could eat this all fall!

1 pound butternut squash cubes

1 red onion, sliced

pinch of dried sage

about 1 tablespoon olive oil

½ cup chopped pecans

¼ cup dried cherries

¼ cup crumbled blue cheese

salt and pepper

VEGETARIAN, GLUTEN-FREE

Preheat oven to 400°F. Arrange squash cubes and sliced onions in a single layer on a rimmed baking sheet. Season with salt, pepper, and sage, and drizzle with olive oil. Roast 15 minutes. Scatter pecans over the top and roast another 5 minutes. Remove squash from oven and toss with dried cherries and blue cheese. Adjust seasonings to taste.

Serves: 4
Prep Time: 5 minutes
Cooking Time: 20 minutes

ROASTED PUMPKIN and GREEN BEANS with PROSCIUTTO and PARMESAN

A beautiful and tasty vegetable dish, but this is also wonderful with pasta, or over polenta, or on top of arugula or other salad greens.

1 small pie pumpkin, peeled and cut into 1-inch cubes

½ pound haricots verts (French green beans) or, if using thicker beans, cut into 3-inch pieces

1 tablespoon olive oil, for drizzling

4 strips prosciutto (or bacon), cut or torn into small pieces

handful of hazelnuts, walnuts, or pecans (optional)

about 1 tablespoon balsamic vinegar

shaved Parmesan cheese, for garnish

salt and pepper

Preheat oven to 400°F. Arrange the pumpkin cubes and green beans on a rimmed baking sheet and drizzle with olive oil. Season with salt and pepper. Scatter the prosciutto over the vegetables and roast until vegetables are tender, about 20 minutes. (If using nuts, add them to the vegetables for the final 5 minutes of roasting.) Remove to a serving dish, drizzle with balsamic vinegar and scatter shaved Parmesan over the top.

Serves: 4 to 6
Prep Time: 15 minutes
Cooking Time: 20 minutes

SOUTHERN GREENS *with* PANCETTA *and* WHITE BEANS

These are southern greens with a Tuscan 'tude.

1 tablespoon olive oil

3 cubes frozen crushed garlic

1 (4-ounce) package diced pancetta

1 (16-ounce) bag Southern Greens Blend, coarsely chopped

1 cup broth (chicken, beef, or vegetable) or water

1 can Trader Joe's Cannellini (White Kidney Beans), drained

salt and pepper

pinch of red chile pepper flakes

GLUTEN-FREE

In a large sauté pan, heat the olive oil and sauté the garlic over medium-high heat for 1 to 2 minutes. Add the pancetta and sauté another 3 to 4 minutes. Add half the bag of greens and sauté until wilted, 3 to 4 minutes. Add the remaining greens and sauté briefly to wilt slightly. Add the broth or water and cook the greens, stirring frequently, until tender, about 8 minutes. Stir in the cannellini beans and season to taste with salt, pepper, and red chile pepper flakes.

Serves: 4 to 6
Prep Time: 5 minutes
Cooking Time: 20 minutes

MUSHROOM MARSALA SAUCE

This sauce is so deeply flavorful, you'll find a million ways to use it. We've served this in the cooking school with roasted pork, with pasta or polenta, or on top of greens as a warm winter salad.

¼ cup dried mushrooms (Trader Joe's Mixed Wild Mushroom Medley)

2 tablespoons olive oil

2 tablespoons butter

4 shallots, minced

1 pound fresh mushrooms, sliced (see note)

3 ounces (half can) tomato paste

salt and pepper

½ cup Marsala

1 cup chicken or vegetable broth

VEGETARIAN *(if made with vegetable broth)*, CLUTEN-FREE

Soak the dried mushrooms in enough hot water to cover until they are softened, about 20 minutes. Strain, reserving the soaking liquid. Coarsely chop the mushrooms and set aside.

Heat oil and butter in large skillet over medium heat, add shallots, and sauté until tender, about 5 minutes. Add the reconstituted dried mushrooms and the fresh mushrooms to the shallots, and sauté until mushrooms are dry and softened, about 5 minutes. Add the tomato paste and sauté until the tomato paste coats the mushrooms and begins to glaze the bottom of the pan. Season lightly with salt and pepper. Off the heat, add the Marsala, then return to the heat over a low flame and simmer until dry, 2 to 3 minutes. Add the reserved soaking liquid from the mushrooms and the chicken or vegetable stock. Bring to a boil, reduce heat and simmer, covered, about 10 minutes. Remove the lid and simmer 10 more minutes. Season to taste with salt and pepper.

Serves: 4 to 6
Prep Time: 20 minutes
Cooking Time: 40 minutes

Save some time by using the 1-pound bag of presliced mushrooms. They are already cleaned, which saves even more time.

AUTUMN SQUASH with CHILI FLAVORS

 Hands-down, one of our most popular recipes at the cooking school. Great flavor and fabulous colors on the plate.

4 cups butternut squash, acorn squash, or pumpkin cubes (or a combination)

1 red onion, thinly sliced

salt and pepper

pinch of red chile pepper flakes

about 1 tablespoon olive oil

1 (15-ounce) can kidney beans or black beans, drained and rinsed

1 (4-ounce) can Trader Joe's Hatch Valley Fire-Roasted Diced Green Chiles

1 cup corn kernels, fresh or frozen and thawed

1½ cups grated cheese (Monterey Jack or Trader Joe's Fancy Shredded Mexican Blend)

VEGETARIAN, GLUTEN-FREE

Preheat oven to 400°F. Place the squash cubes and red onion on a rimmed baking sheet, and season with salt, pepper, and red chile pepper flakes. Drizzle with olive oil and roast until squash is tender, about 18 to 20 minutes. Remove to a serving dish and toss with drained beans, chiles, corn, and cheese. Adjust seasoning to taste with salt and pepper.

Serves: 4
Prep Time: 10 minutes
Cooking Time: 25 minutes

SPICY CORNY GREEN BEANS

This one's great any way you serve it—hot, at room temperature, or chilled!

2 (8-ounce) bags fresh haricots verts (French green beans) or 1 pound regular green beans, trimmed and cut into 3-inch lengths

½ (13.75-ounce) jar Trader Joe's Corn and Chile Tomato-Less Salsa

¼ to ½ cup crumbled feta cheese

VEGETARIAN, GLUTEN-FREE

Steam or boil the green beans until barely tender, 6 to 10 minutes. While hot, toss with corn salsa and top with crumbled feta cheese.

Serves: 4
Prep Time: 5 minutes
Cooking Time: 10 minutes

SASSY PEACH SWEET POTATOES

You won't believe how good these can be until you try them. The combination of vibrant color and zingy, spicy flavors can't be beat.

1 tablespoon olive oil

1 red onion, sliced

4 cubes frozen crushed garlic

4 medium sweet potatoes, peeled and cubed

1½ cups chicken broth

1 (12-ounce) jar Trader Joe's Spicy, Smoky Peach Salsa

salt and pepper

VEGETARIAN, GLUTEN-FREE

In a large sauté pan, heat the oil and sauté the onion over medium-high heat until tender, about 5 minutes. Add the garlic and sauté until fragrant, 2 to 3 minutes. Add the sweet potato cubes and sauté 3 to 4 minutes. Add the chicken broth and salsa. Bring to a boil, reduce heat, cover, and simmer until sweet potatoes are nearly tender, 10 to 15 minutes. Remove cover, and if there is still a lot of liquid, increase the heat to high and boil until the liquid is reduced to a glaze. Season to taste with salt and pepper.

Serves: 4
Prep Time: 10 minutes
Cooking Time: 30 minutes

MASHED SWEET POTATOES

My kids are not big sweet potato fans, but they devour these. You can substitute some goat cheese for the crème fraîche, too.

3 pounds sweet potatoes, peeled and cubed

¼ cup crème fraîche

2 tablespoons butter

2 cubes frozen crushed garlic

salt and pepper

dash of Trader Joe's Chili Pepper Hot Sauce or Jalapeño Pepper Hot Sauce

VEGETARIAN, GLUTEN-FREE

Place sweet potatoes in a medium saucepan and cover with water. Bring to a boil, reduce heat, and simmer until potatoes are tender, about 15 minutes. (Cooking time will depend on the size of the sweet potato cubes.) Drain the potatoes and return them to the pan. Add the crème fraîche, butter, and garlic, and stir until melted. Mash the potatoes into this mixture until smooth. Season to taste with salt, pepper, and hot pepper sauce.

Serves: 4 to 6

Prep Time: 10 minutes

Cooking Time: 20 minutes

• •

Thinned with a vegetable or chicken broth, this makes a great soup. Just add about a cup of broth after you mash the sweet potatoes, season to taste, and stir over medium heat until the mixture is smooth.

• •

GREEN BEANS
with MUSHROOM BRIE

These are terrific on a holiday table. Garnished with some Trader Joe's Gourmet Fried Onion Pieces or even some of Joe's great pomegranate arils, they look as festive as they are delicious.

1 pound green beans, trimmed

1 tablespoon butter or olive oil

3 ounces sliced mushrooms

¼ cup heavy cream or crème fraîche

6 ounces Champignon Brie, cubed

Trader Joe's Gourmet Fried Onion Pieces and/or pomegranate arils, for garnish (optional)

salt and freshly ground pepper

VEGETARIAN, GLUTEN-FREE *(if made without the fried onions)*

Cook the green beans in rapidly boiling, salted water until crisp-tender, 6 to 8 minutes. Heat the butter or olive oil in a medium sauté pan, and sauté the mushrooms over medium-high heat until softened, about 6 minutes. Toss mushrooms with green beans. Warm the cream or crème fraîche in a small saucepan, and then add the Brie, stirring until melted. Pour sauce over green beans and mushrooms, and toss to combine. Adjust seasoning with salt and pepper. Garnish with fried onions or pomegranate arils, if desired.

Serves: 4

Prep Time: 5 minutes

Cooking Time: 15 minutes

This is great with asparagus, in addition to the beans or as a substitute.

PECAN GREEN BEANS

The pecan vinaigrette is fast and flavorful, and the nuttiness is great with the beans.

1 (10-ounce) bag green beans or mixed green and yellow beans (in fresh produce area)

½ cup pecan halves

2 tablespoons red wine vinegar

½ cup olive oil or canola oil

salt and freshly ground black pepper

VEGETARIAN, VEGAN

In a medium saucepan of salted, boiling water, cook the beans until crisp-tender, 6 to 8 minutes. Drain and set aside. In a small sauté pan, toast the pecan halves over medium heat until slightly browned and aromatic. Remove about 2 tablespoons of pecan halves, chop coarsely, and set aside. Place the rest of the pecans in a food processor or blender, add the vinegar, and process until the nuts are finely chopped. Add the oil in a steady stream while the motor is running. Toss the dressing with the beans and season to taste with salt and pepper. Garnish with chopped pecans.

Serves: 2 to 3
Prep Time: 5 minutes
Cooking Time: less than 10 minutes

SCALLOPED CORN

An old-fashioned technique for corn, but there's nothing outdated about the taste.

2 tablespoons butter

1 shallot, thinly sliced

½ red bell pepper, chopped

3 cups fresh or frozen corn kernels

½ cup heavy cream

¼ teaspoon dried thyme or 1 teaspoon fresh thyme

salt and pepper

½ cup fresh bread crumbs

¼ cup grated Parmesan cheese

VEGETARIAN

Preheat oven to 350°F. In a small sauté pan, melt the butter and sauté the shallot and red pepper over medium-high heat for about 4 minutes, or until softened. In a medium bowl, combine the sautéed pepper and shallot with the corn, cream, thyme, and some salt and pepper, to taste. Place in an ovenproof casserole. Combine the bread crumbs and Parmesan cheese and sprinkle over the top of the corn mixture. Bake about 20 minutes, until bubbling and warmed through.

Serves: 4

Prep Time: 5 minutes

Cooking Time: 25 minutes

END of the SEASON GREEN BEAN SALAD

The nuttiness of the artichokes pairs well with the slightly bitter edge of the walnuts. This dish is great at the end of summer, when we are about to say goodbye to great green beans for the year.

½ pound green beans, ends trimmed off

½ cup walnut pieces

½ cup marinated artichoke hearts

2 teaspoons red wine vinegar

2 tablespoons olive oil

2 ounces goat cheese (Trader Joe's Chèvre, Silver Goat Chèvre, or Madame Chèvre)

salt and pepper

VEGETARIAN

Drain the artichokes on a paper towel to remove most of marinade. Steam the green beans until just crisp-tender, 6 to 8 minutes. Place in a bowl. Toast the walnut pieces in a dry sauté pan over medium heat until slightly browned and aromatic. Add to the green beans. Place the artichoke hearts in the same sauté pan and sauté until the edges of the leaves take on a grilled or charred appearance, 2 to 3 minutes. Add to bowl. Pour the vinegar and oil over the cooked vegetables and toss to coat. Let stand 10 minutes so the vegetables absorb some of the dressing. Crumble the goat cheese over the vegetables and adjust seasonings to taste with salt and pepper.

Serves: 2 to 3
Prep Time: 5 minutes
Cooking Time: 15 minutes

Chapter 11

DESSERTS

Dessert is back. For decades, the dessert course was forsaken in the United States—or eaten with a hearty helping of guilt or justification. But I think the cupcake craze has started to bring dessert back. There are several dessert-only restaurants in my area now, and I say hooray! A little something sweet—I'm talking a two- or three-bite treat—can lift your spirits like nothing else.

Most of the desserts in this chapter are based on fruit or contain dark chocolate, and we all know those are full of healthful antioxidants. So they're practically health food, right? While I may be stretching the point a wee bit, I do think that dessert, in moderation, is good for our emotional well-being. A little frippery can brighten an otherwise dull day, and who doesn't appreciate that?

With the new sweeteners on the shelves at Trader Joe's these days, you can play with substituting agave syrup or stevia for sugar in your sweets and feel better about them than the processed sugar-bombs available in some places. Anything you make from these pages will have ingredients you can pronounce, unlike some of the stuff from the prepared-food sections or frozen-food aisles of other stores, which tend to be pumped full of preservatives and chemicals. Compare the ingredients in the amazing Trader Joe's frozen Artisan Puff Pastry with the puff pastry in the freezer section at other stores. They're like night and day—the TJ's ingredients are far superior, and it shows in the finished product. I don't even want to tell you how many boxes of this divine stuff I have in my freezer at any given moment. It's currently stocked seasonally, so hoard it like mad during the holidays, and use it all year. Slap some seasonal, sliced fruit on top, sprinkle with some turbinado sugar or stevia, and pop it in the hot oven for a fragrant and fabulous homemade treat that looks like it came straight out of a pink bakery box!

If time is short, you can always skip these recipes and plunder the frozen-food case at Joe's for some great prepared goodies. My gymnast daughter used to devour the Trader Joe's Gone Bananas! chocolate-dipped frozen bananas (known as "fro-ban" in our house) by the boxful. I know a certain Joe who recommends eating the frozen carrot cake while it's still frozen—just grab a spoon and dig in! I can't say enough about the frozen Raspberry Crème Brûlées. They're made in France, where they know how to brûlée their crème, and they comes in the most completely adorable little terra-cotta ramekins, which you get to *keep afterward!* I use these shallow custard cups for olives, almonds, for making an array of tapas, and even to hold paper clips on my cluttered desk. So, basically, in each package you are purchasing two very useful pieces of serving ware for $2.50, and they just happen to come filled with creamy berryliciousness. Plus, you are saving the planet with your clever recycling ideas. Talk about a bargain! If that doesn't make you feel good about dessert, I don't know what will.

BLACKBERRY FOOL

Why don't we make fools anymore? Basically, they are puréed fruit with whipped cream. So simple but so tasty.

1 (12-ounce) container fresh blackberries (frozen will work, too)

⅔ cup sugar, divided

squeeze of lemon juice

1½ cups heavy cream

VEGETARIAN, GLUTEN-FREE

In a food processor, purée the berries. Add ⅓ cup sugar (use less if using sweetened, frozen berries) and lemon juice, and blend. In a separate bowl, with an electric mixer or whisk, beat the cream until it holds a peak when the beater (or whisk) is lifted from the bowl. Add the remaining sugar gradually as the cream whips. Blend in the purée. Spoon into individual glasses and chill or freeze.

Serves: 4
Prep Time: 5 minutes
Cooking Time: none

This is terrific served in simple glasses, or kick it up by spooning it into chocolate cups or puff pastry shells. To make these, use a round 2½- to 3-inch cookie cutter to cut circles out of a sheet of puff pastry. Then use a smaller cutter (or a knife) to inscribe a smaller concentric circle on the dough, but don't cut all the way through the pastry with this one. Place the dough rounds on a parchment-lined baking sheet and place in a preheated 400°F oven for about 18 minutes, until puffed and golden. Cool slightly, and, using the tip of a knife, lift out the center circle of crust and any slightly underbaked dough. Voila—puff pastry shells that can be used for sweet or savory fillings.

RASPBERRY CARAMEL TURNOVERS

These are great do-aheads, and you can keep them in the fridge for a few days before baking or freeze them and bake a few at a time when you need a sweet treat.

1 package Trader Joe's frozen Artisan Puff Pastry, thawed but kept cold

1 (17.5-ounce) jar Trader Joe's Fresh Raspberry Preserves

5 caramels from a 10-ounce container Trader Joe's Dark Chocolate Covered Caramels, cut in half (you'll have a half left over for quality control!)

VEGETARIAN.

Preheat oven to 400°F. Roll the pastry out a bit, and cut into nine 3-inch squares. Spread the pastry with about a teaspoonful of raspberry preserves and place half a caramel in the center. Fold the pastry, corner to corner, to form a triangle, and press the edges with a fork to seal. Chill 15 minutes in freezer. Bake until pastry is golden, 18 to 20 minutes. Cool slightly before eating—the filling is very hot!

Serves: 9
Prep Time: 15 minutes
Cooking Time: 20 minutes

HAIRDRESSER BLONDIES

One day, my "hair goddess," Christine, had a small plastic bag full of homemade trail mix at her station. It had almonds, chocolate chips, and the amazing dried Rainier cherries in it. Those Rainier cherries are beyond belief, with an almost caramelly, deep, rich flavor and they're wonderful in this recipe. If they are not available, dried Bing cherries will do.

2 cups Trader Joe's Multigrain
Baking and Pancake Mix

1 cup brown sugar

½ cup melted butter

1 egg

2 teaspoons vanilla

⅓ cup Trader Joe's Dried
Rainier Cherries (or other dried
cherries), coarsely chopped

½ cup dry-roasted (salted or
unsalted) almonds, chopped

½ cup semisweet chocolate chips

VEGETARIAN

Preheat oven to 350°F. Butter or spray an 8-inch cake pan or tart pan with a removable bottom. In a bowl, combine the baking mix, brown sugar, melted butter, egg, and vanilla. Stir to combine. Add the chopped dried cherries, almonds, and chocolate chips, and stir to incorporate. Spread the batter in prepared pan and bake until cooked through, about 30 minutes.

Serves: 12
Prep Time: 10 minutes
Cooking Time: 30 minutes

I can't stress enough the fabulousness of those Rainier cherries. I haunt the dried fruit section as summer nears, and if I see them, you *know* I grab armfuls. What can I say? I'm a hoarder when it comes to Joe's best stuff!

SILKY, SINFUL CHOCOLATE TART

TJ's pie crust is amazing. I encourage students to leave the rolling pin out on the counter with little bits of dough clinging to it. Everyone will assume you made the crust yourself, and I see no reason to contradict that assumption!

1 Trader Joe's Gourmet Pie Crust (in the frozen-food section), defrosted (refreeze the remaining one for another use)

2 to 3 tablespoons Trader Joe's Fresh Raspberry Preserves (or another flavor)

8 ounces Trader Joe's Dark Chocolate, chopped

1¼ cup heavy cream

1 egg

2 egg yolks

3 tablespoons butter, at room temperature

1 pint fresh raspberries, for garnish (optional)

½ (7.5-ounce) container of crème fraîche, softly whipped and slightly sweetened, for garnish (optional)

VEGETARIAN

Preheat oven to 400°F. Roll the pie dough out a little and fit it into an 8- or 9-inch tart pan with a removable bottom. Cover with crinkled parchment, then add a layer of pie weights (or dried beans or raw rice). Bake 12 minutes, carefully remove parchment along with weights (or beans or rice), and bake an additional 5 to 7 minutes, until the dough loses its wet appearance. Cool to room temperature. Spoon the preserves onto the crust and spread evenly.

Place the chopped chocolate in a heatproof bowl. In a small saucepan, heat the cream over low heat to a simmer, then pour the hot cream over the chocolate. Stir until the chocolate melts and combines evenly with the cream. In a separate bowl, stir together the whole egg and yolks, then add about half the warm chocolate and cream mixture, stirring. (This is called *tempering*, and it prevents the eggs from scrambling.) Add this mixture back into the chocolate and stir to combine well. Add the butter and stir to combine. Pour into the baked tart crust on top of the preserves and return to the oven for 18 minutes. The center of the tart will appear to be barely set, but it will firm up as it cools. Allow to cool at least 30 minutes before serving. Garnish with fresh raspberries and whipped crème fraîche, if desired. This tart is quite rich, so slice it thinly.

Serves: 8

Prep Time: 5 minutes

Cooking Time: less than an hour, plus cooling time

. . . .

Crème fraîche is perfect when you want something a little less sweet than whipped cream. Place the crème fraîche in a bowl; beat with a wire whisk until it billows with soft peaks. You can sweeten it, if you like, with a tablespoon or two of sugar or agave syrup.

. . . .

BERRY-ZIN SAUCE

I took cooking classes years ago from a wonderful cooking teacher, Hugh Carpenter. Hugh has written many great cookbooks and teaches classes in Napa, California. This is a variation on a dessert sauce from one of his classes that I've made for decades. The whole house will smell amazing as this simmers. It's great on ice cream, on pound cake, or as a finishing dessert sauce for cakes. In theory, it lasts at least a week in the refrigerator. In practice (at least at my house), it doesn't last nearly that long.

1 bottle Zinfandel (drinkable but not expensive)

1 (16-ounce) bag frozen Fancy Berry Medley (or 12-ounce bag of frozen raspberries)

1 cup sugar

several grinds of black pepper

VEGETARIAN, VEGAN, GLUTEN-FREE

Place all ingredients in a sauté pan (not a saucepan—you want more surface area for more efficient reduction) and bring to a boil. Reduce heat and simmer about 30 minutes, until mixture is reduced to 2 cups. Strain through a sieve to remove seeds.

Prep Time: 5 minutes
Cooking Time: 30 minutes

GINGERBREAD *with* MASCARPONE *and* PEARS

The gingerbread mix is seasonal, so stock up, because as far as I'm concerned, it's always the right season for this treat!

butter or spray oil

1 box Trader Joe's Deep, Dark Gingerbread and Baking Mix

1 egg

½ (8-ounce) container mascarpone

¼ cup sugar

1 cup ripe pears, chopped

VEGETARIAN

Preheat oven to 350°F. Prepare the gingerbread batter according to package directions. Lightly butter or spray an 8-inch baking pan and spread half the gingerbread batter into the pan. Stir together the egg, mascarpone, sugar, and pears. Scatter dollops of the mascarpone mixture into the gingerbread batter. Cover with the remaining gingerbread batter. Bake until a skewer inserted into the gingerbread comes out clean, about 35 minutes. (If the skewer comes out with mascarpone on it, try a different spot.)

Serves: 8
Prep Time: 5 minutes
Cooking Time: 35 minutes

• •

For a charming variation, slice the pears and arrange them on the bottom of the cake pan in a spiral pattern. Spoon the gingerbread batter on top and bake. The pretty pear pattern will then be on top. Whisk together the mascarpone and sugar, then dollop the mixture on slices of the baked, unmolded cake.

• •

This gingerbread mix contains cocoa, so beware if you are serving someone with an allergy issue.

• •

BETTER-THAN-TIRAMISU

Such a quick and easy dessert to make when berries are gorgeous! Ladyfingers are "seasonal" at TJ's—what season IS ladyfinger season, I wonder? Apparently it's winter, so stock up so you'll be sure to have enough to last all year!

1 (10.5-ounce) jar Trader Joe's Lemon Curd

1½ (8-ounce) containers mascarpone

1 tablespoon frozen fruit juice (orange or another complementary flavor of your choice) defrosted but not diluted

2 tablespoons Grand Marnier or other citrus liqueur

1 package Trader Joe's Soft Lady Fingers

about 2 cups fresh berries (if using strawberries, hulled and sliced)

VEGETARIAN

With an electric mixer (or by hand), beat the lemon curd just enough to lighten the texture. Add the mascarpone and beat until combined, being careful not to overbeat. (The mascarpone can become grainy quickly if overbeaten, so be careful if using a mixer—just a few seconds will do the trick.) Set aside. Combine the juice concentrate and Grand Marnier in a small bowl. Dip the flat side of each ladyfinger into the mixture and place half of them, dipped side up, in a 8 x 8-inch casserole dish. Spread half the lemon curd–mascarpone mixture over the ladyfingers and top with half the berries. Repeat the dipping and layering of ladyfingers, top with the remaining lemon curd–mascarpone mixture, then add the rest of the berries. Cover with plastic wrap and refrigerate at least 1 hour.

Serves: 6

Prep Time: 10 minutes

Cooking Time: none

Don't use berries that aren't gorgeous. If peaches or nectarines are lovelier, use those, peeled and sliced.

TJ'S TRIFLE

This can be thrown together in just a few minutes, but the flavor is terrific.

1 package Triple Ginger Snaps (or another favorite cookie)

1 cup heavy cream

1 (8-ounce) container mascarpone

2 tablespoons Chambord black raspberry liqueur

1 to 2 tablespoons sugar

2 cups strawberries, raspberries, blackberries, or blueberries, or a combination (sweetened to taste, if needed)

VEGETARIAN

Pulverize the cookies into crumbs using a food processor (or put them in a large double resealable plastic bag and crush them with a rolling pin) and set aside. Whip the cream to soft peaks, sweetening with sugar, as desired. Stir in the Chambord and then add the mascarpone, stirring to combine. In individual glasses or a large glass dish, layer some of the cream-mascarpone mixture, some berries, and some cookie crumbs. Repeat until you have three or four layers, ending with the cookie crumbs.

Serves: 6

Prep Time: 15 minutes

Cooking Time: none

DOUBLE BLACKBERRY TART

The flavors of blackberries and almonds go so well together. A scoop of the terrific TJ's vanilla ice cream would put this over the top.

1 Trader Joe's Gourmet Pie Crust, defrosted (refreeze the remaining one for another use)

1½ cups blanched, slivered almonds

½ cup sugar

4 ounces butter

2 eggs

¼ teaspoon vanilla

1 tablespoon flour

¼ cup Trader Joe's Blackberry Preserves

1½ cups fresh blackberries

vanilla ice cream (optional)

VEGETARIAN

Preheat oven to 375°F. Roll pie dough, if needed to repair cracks, and press into a 9-inch tart tin or pie pan. Chill the crust while the filling is prepared. Place the almonds in a food processor and pulse to chop. Add the sugar and process until powdered. Add butter and blend to combine. Add eggs, vanilla, and flour and process again to combine.

Spread the preserves on the bottom of the unbaked pastry shell. Cover with the almond mixture, spreading carefully and evenly. Arrange the blackberries on top and bake the tart until it is set and fragrant, about 35 minutes. Serve and top with ice cream, if desired.

Serves: 8
Prep Time: 10 minutes
Cooking Time: 35 minutes

BREAD PUDDING *with* BOURBON SAUCE

As my dear friend Bob would say, this rich dessert is "slap yo' momma good!"

BOURBON SAUCE:

1 egg

⅓ cup granulated sugar

⅓ cup brown sugar

¼ cup water

4 tablespoons butter

¼ cup bourbon

BREAD PUDDING:

8 cups bread cubes made from about eight day-old croissants

½ cup raisins, Trader Joe's Golden Berry Blend, or chocolate chips

3 eggs

½ cup granulated sugar

⅓ cup brown sugar

2 cups milk

1 cup heavy cream

1 tablespoon vanilla

½ teaspoon cinnamon

VEGETARIAN

FOR SAUCE: In a medium bowl, beat the egg with a fork to combine the white and yolk well. Set aside. In a small saucepan, combine the sugars, water, and butter. Bring to a simmer, and cook until the sugar is dissolved. Pour about a third of this mixture into the beaten egg, whisking rapidly as you pour. (This will help to prevent the eggs from scrambling.) Then return that mixture to the saucepan and cook over low heat, stirring, about 2 minutes, until sauce thickens. Remove the pan from the heat and stir in the bourbon. The bourbon sauce can be made several hours, or even a day, ahead and then refrigerated. (Rewarm before serving.)

FOR BREAD PUDDING: Preheat oven to 325°F. Butter a 2-quart baking dish or about eight ramekins. Toss the bread with the raisins, berries, or chocolate chips in a large bowl. Whisk together the remaining ingredients and pour over the bread. Cover with plastic wrap and weight down, if necessary, to immerse the bread in the egg mixture, or stir occasionally. Let stand 15 minutes.

Place the bread mixture into the prepared dish(es). Bake 30 minutes (for ramekins) to 1 hour (for 2-quart dish). When done, the top will be golden brown, and a knife inserted into the center should come out clean. Cool slightly before serving with bourbon sauce on top.

Serves: 8

Prep Time: 10 minutes

Cooking Time: 30 to 60 minutes

CHERRY-BERRY CRISP

This smells heavenly as it bakes, and tastes even better, if that's possible.

2 (16-ounce) bags Very Cherry Berry Blend (frozen berries with no strawberries)

¼ cup powdered sugar

½ cup Trader Joe's Multigrain Baking and Pancake Mix

½ cup brown sugar

½ cup McCann's Quick Cooking Irish Oatmeal

¼ cup butter

½ cup nuts (hazelnuts, pecans, walnuts, or whatever you like)

about ½ cup Fage Total Yogurt and maple syrup or honey (optional)

VEGETARIAN

Preheat oven to 375°F. Combine the berries and powdered sugar in a 2-quart ovenproof casserole and set aside. In a food processor, combine the rest of the ingredients and pulse to combine coarsely. Place this mixture on top of the berries and bake until bubbly, about 30 minutes. Cool 5 to 10 minutes before serving. Top individual servings with yogurt sweetened to taste with maple syrup or honey, if desired.

Serves: 6
Prep Time: 5 minutes
Cooking Time: 30 minutes

• •

You can vary the frozen fruit for different flavor combinations. Peaches (fresh or frozen) and some chopped crystallized ginger are terrific! I prefer not to use frozen strawberries because they tend to exude more water than other fruits.

• •

ALMOND-PLUM GALETTE

This is great with a combination of pears and raspberries in place of the plums. Use whatever looks great in the fruit aisle.

⅔ cup blanched, slivered almonds

3 ounces butter

½ cup brown sugar

2 eggs

1 tablespoon flour

zest of 1 lemon

1 teaspoon almond or vanilla extract

1 Trader Joe's Gourmet Pie Crust (in the frozen-food section), defrosted (refreeze the remaining one for another use)

4 plums, sliced

2 tablespoons turbinado sugar, for garnish (optional)

handful of slivered almonds, for garnish (optional)

VEGETARIAN

Preheat oven to 375°F. Place the almonds in a food processor and pulse to grind the nuts to a powder. Remove to a bowl and set aside. Place butter and sugar in the processor and blend until light and thoroughly combined. Add one egg and process to combine. Add the second egg and repeat. Add the ground almonds and the flour, and process just until combined. Add the almond or vanilla extract and lemon zest and combine. Chill in refrigerator for 30 minutes or in freezer 15 minutes. Roll the pie dough with a rolling pin, if necessary to repair cracks. Place on a parchment-lined baking sheet. Spread the filling onto the center of the pie crust, leaving a 2-inch border of pastry uncovered. Arrange the plum slices in a pretty pattern over the top and fold the pastry edges in, on top of the filling, leaving the center of the filling exposed. Bake until puffed and golden, about 25 minutes. (If desired, sprinkle crunchy sugar, such as turbinado, or sliced almonds over the top of the tart in the last 5 minutes of baking.)

Serves: 8
Prep Time: 10 minutes
Cooking Time: 25 minutes

MINI VANILLA WAFER CHEESECAKES

This recipe is just waiting to be played around with. Pop some berries in before you bake them, or maybe a little piece of caramel. Crushed gingersnaps would be great as the base, too.

12 Trader Joe's Ultimate Vanilla Wafers

½ cup sugar

2 eggs

8 ounces cream cheese, at room temperature

8 ounces mascarpone, at room temperature

1 teaspoon vanilla

zest of 1 lemon

12 fresh berries and Trader Joe's Wild Maine Blueberry Fruit Sauce, for garnish

VEGETARIAN

Preheat oven to 325°F. Place paper liners in a 12-hole muffin pan and place a vanilla wafer in the bottom of each. With an electric mixer, combine the sugar and eggs, then add the cream cheese, mascarpone, vanilla, and lemon zest, and mix to combine. Pour over the vanilla wafers, dividing evenly. Bake until set, 20 to 25 minutes. Cool before serving. Top each mini-cheesecake with a fresh berry and drizzle with blueberry sauce.

Serves: 12

Prep Time: 10 minutes

Cooking Time: 25 minutes

TUMBLE-FRUIT CRUMBLE

This is a great way to use whatever fruit is gorgeous at the moment. I double or triple the crumble topping and store the leftovers in the freezer so I can tumble together the fruit and topping on the spur of the moment.

3 to 4 cups ripe fruit (apricots, plums, nectarines, peaches, berries, or apples are all good)

2 tablespoons to ¼ cup Trader Joe's Organic Blue Agave Sweetener or brown sugar (see note)

CRUMBLE TOPPING:

½ cup flour

½ cup brown sugar

4 tablespoons butter (cold)

¼ cup rolled oats

½ cup chopped pecans

½ teaspoon cinnamon

VEGETARIAN

Preheat oven to 400°F. Cut fruit into bite-sized pieces and toss with agave syrup or brown sugar to desired degree of sweetness.

FOR CRUMBLE TOPPING: In a food processor, mix the flour, brown sugar, butter, oats, pecans, and cinnamon until barely combined. Place fruit in a 6 cup soufflé dish or deep-dish pie pan and cover with crumble topping. Bake 20 to 25 minutes, until the topping is browned and fragrant and the filling is bubbling.

Serves: 6 to 8

Prep Time: 10 minutes

Cooking Time: 25 minutes

Fruit that is quite tart, such as raspberries and plums, may require more sweetening than very ripe peaches or nectarines.

PUFF PASTRY PILLOWS

Feel free to experiment with this recipe. In place of the yogurt cheese and preserves, you could use mascarpone or lemon curd, and use whatever fruit is gorgeous.

1 package Trader Joe's frozen Artisan Puff Pastry, defrosted but kept cold

½ cup turbinado sugar

1 (16-ounce) container Mediterranean Cheese Style Yogurt

½ cup Trader Joe's Fresh Apricot Preserves (or to taste)

about 6 ripe apricots, thinly sliced

1 to 2 tablespoons honey (optional)

1 pint blueberries or raspberries, for garnish (optional)

VEGETARIAN

Preheat oven to 400°F. (Use convection oven, if you have it.) Line a baking sheet with parchment. Sprinkle a good handful of the turbinado sugar onto a work surface and lay a sheet of puff pastry on top. Sprinkle more sugar on the top of the pastry and roll a rolling pin across the pastry, just enough to press the sugar into the pastry. Cut pastry into desired shapes and sizes. (I usually get nine rectangles out of each sheet.) Repeat with the remaining sheet of pastry if you need more than nine "pillows."

Place the pastry pieces on the baking sheet. Bake until crisp and golden, 12 to 15 minutes. While the pastry cooks, stir together the yogurt cheese and preserves, and taste to see if you like the sweetness. (If the apricots you are using are very sweet, use more yogurt cheese; if the apricots are tart, add more preserves or a little honey to achieve your perfect flavor.)

When the pastry is baked, use a serrated knife to split the "pillows" in half horizontally. Dollop about ¼ cup of the apricot yogurt cheese on each pastry bottom and top with the sliced apricots. Add a few berries, if desired, and place the top half of the pastry on top of the fruit.

Serves: 9
Prep Time: 15 minutes
Cooking Time: 15 minutes

MEYER LEMON RASPBERRY CLOUDS

Meyer lemons are less acidic than regular ones, and their skin is deeply fragrant. If your TJ's doesn't have them in stock, use regular lemons and a little more sugar or some agave syrup.

4 eggs

½ cup sugar

1 cup heavy cream

2 teaspoons Meyer lemon zest

½ cup Meyer lemon juice (from about 2 medium lemons)

1 pint raspberries

VEGETARIAN, GLUTEN-FREE

Preheat the oven to 325°F. Whisk the eggs and sugar together, and then whisk in the cream. Whisk in the lemon zest and juice. Place six ramekins (or custard cups) in a larger baking pan with a high rim, divide the lemon mixture evenly between the ramekins, and add a few raspberries to each ramekin. Place the baking pan in the oven. Fill the baking pan with warm water halfway up the sides of the ramekins. Bake 30 to 40 minutes, or until set but still jiggly. Serve hot, warm, or chilled.

Serves: 6

Prep Time: 15 minutes

Cooking Time: 40 minutes

CHOCOLATE PUMPKIN TART

I've gotten tremendous mileage out of this fast and fabulous holiday dessert. It goes together really quickly and can be dressed up with whipped cream or other frippery.

1 Trader Joe's Gourmet Pie Crust (in the frozen-food section), defrosted (refreeze the remaining one for another use)

1 cup chocolate chips or chopped chocolate

1 (9-ounce) jar Trader Joe's Pumpkin Butter

1 (8-ounce) container mascarpone

1 to 2 tablespoons bourbon (optional)

whipped cream or crème fraîche (optional)

VEGETARIAN

To blind-bake the tart shell: Preheat oven to 375°F. Roll out pie dough and fit into an 8- or 9-inch pie pan or tart pan with a removable bottom. Cover the pastry with crinkled parchment and weigh it down with a layer of pie weights, raw rice, or dried beans. Place in oven for 12 minutes. Carefully remove parchment, with weights inside, and return pan to the oven for 5 to 10 minutes, until pastry is dry and golden.

When the pastry is baked, remove it from the oven and scatter chocolate over the surface. Let stand a few minutes, then spread the melted chocolate evenly over the crust. Stir together the pumpkin butter and mascarpone, adding some bourbon, if desired. Spoon into the baked tart shell and chill 1 hour before serving. Garnish with whipped cream or crème fraîche, if desired.

Serves: 8
Prep Time: 10 minutes
Cooking Time: 25 minutes, plus chilling time

I love the look of one of Trader Joe's Dark Chocolate Stars cookies perched on top of a billow of crème fraîche on top of a slice of this tart. The pumpkin butter and chocolate stars are both seasonal items, so hoard them when you see them.

MAXI-MINI PEANUT BUTTER CUP COOKIES

I'm not much of a peanut butter girl, and there are a million candy bars on the shelf I'd scarf up before I ate a peanut butter cup. But these cookies have something special goin' on, and I've been known to eat several at a time.

3 ounces butter, at room temperature

¼ cup peanut butter

½ cup granulated sugar

⅓ cup dark brown sugar

1 egg

1 teaspoon vanilla

1 cup flour

pinch salt

⅛ teaspoon baking soda

1 cup Trader Joe's Mini Milk Chocolate Peanut Butter Cups

VEGETARIAN

Preheat oven to 375°F. Line a baking sheet with parchment. With an electric mixer, beat the butter with the peanut butter until light, about 2 minutes. Add the granulated and brown sugar and beat to combine well. Add the egg and vanilla and mix well. With a rubber spatula or wooden spoon, stir in the flour, salt, and baking soda until just combined. Add the mini peanut butter cups and stir gently to distribute them well in the batter. Drop by spoonfuls onto the prepared baking sheet and bake until golden, about 12 minutes.

Makes: 1½ dozen
Prep Time: 10 minutes
Cooking Time: 12 minutes

Consider making decadent ice cream sandwiches with these cookies and TJ's terrific vanilla ice cream.

PUMPKIN CRANBERRY CAKE *with* PUMPKIN BUTTER-MASCARPONE SLATHER

Terrific with a cup of tea in the afternoon or for a lunchbox treat.

1 package Trader Joe's Pumpkin Bread and Muffin Mix

2 eggs

½ cup canola oil

1 cup cranberry juice

½ cup dried cranberries

1 container Trader Joe's Pumpkin Butter

1 (8-ounce) container mascarpone

honey and/or bourbon (optional)

VEGETARIAN

Preheat oven to 350°F. Lightly oil an 8- or 9-inch cake pan, or spray it with baking spray. Place the pumpkin bread mix in a large bowl. In a small bowl, stir together the eggs, oil, and cranberry juice, then add this mixture to the pumpkin bread mix, stirring to combine. Stir in dried cranberries and pour the mixture into the prepared pan. Bake until a skewer or knife blade inserted in the center comes out clean, 30 to 40 minutes.

Stir together the pumpkin butter and mascarpone. Flavor with bourbon and/or sweeten with honey, if desired. Pipe or spoon a dollop of the fluffy sauce on each slice of cake to serve.

Serves: 6
Prep Time: 5 minutes
Cooking Time: 40 minutes

Both the pumpkin butter and the pumpkin bread mix are seasonal, so be sure to hoard enough to last you through the year!

QUICK ALMOND CAKE

 This is similar to a French housewife's favorite home-baked treat. The yogurt adds moisture, tenderness, and tang to the cake, and the raspberry preserves add another layer of flavor.

½ cup Trader Joe's Just Almond Meal

1 cup flour

2 teaspoons baking powder

pinch of salt

1 cup sugar

½ cup plain yogurt

3 eggs

½ teaspoon almond extract

½ cup canola oil

½ cup Trader Joe's Fresh Raspberry Preserves (or apricot preserves, or just about any fruit jam you like!)

VEGETARIAN

Preheat oven to 350°F. Butter a 9-inch cake pan and set aside. In a medium bowl, combine the almond meal, flour, baking powder, and salt, and set aside. Place the sugar in the bowl of an electric mixer and combine with the yogurt, eggs, and almond extract. Stir in the dry ingredients, and then add the canola oil. Stir until incorporated and pour the batter into the prepared pan. Bake until the cake is golden and slightly pulling away from the sides of the pan, about 25 minutes. Cool 10 minutes in the pan before unmolding. Melt the preserves in a saucepan (or the microwave) until spreadable, and spread on top of the cake.

Serves: 8
Prep Time: 10 minutes
Cooking Time: 25 minutes

HAZELNUT-PLUM BABY CAKES

I love the idea of individual cakes that bake up so quickly and taste so satisfying. Of course, you can use other fruit as well. I still mourn the discontinuation of the vanilla paste Trader Joe's used to carry, so I'm repeating my pleas for a write-in campaign!

2 plums

¾ cup hazelnuts (or slivered almonds)

½ cup butter

½ cup sugar

2 eggs

1 teaspoon vanilla extract or paste

⅓ cup flour

VEGETARIAN

Preheat the oven to 400°F. Cut the plums in half and remove pits. Place half a plum, cut side down, in each of four ovenproof ramekins. In a food processor, finely chop the hazelnuts (or almonds). Set aside. Place the butter and sugar in the food processor, and blend until smooth. Add the eggs, vanilla extract, flour, and the chopped nuts and pulse just until combined. Spoon batter over the plums, dividing evenly among the ramekins. Smooth the surface and bake until golden, about 20 minutes.

Serves: 4
Prep Time: 10 minutes
Cooking Time: 20 minutes

ALMOND-AGAVE BABY CAKES

I've been having fun playing with the new agave syrup at TJ's. It has a rich, caramelly undernote, and it's great for baking. I also love it as a sweetener for lemonade or iced tea because it doesn't sink to the bottom of the glass like regular sugar.

4 tablespoons butter (plus additional for prepping pan)

2 eggs

⅓ cup Trader Joe's Organic Blue Agave Sweetener

pinch of salt

1 teaspoon vanilla

½ cup flour

¼ cup Trader Joe's Just Almond Meal

12 berries (optional)

about ¼ cup powdered sugar, for garnish (optional)

VEGETARIAN

Preheat oven to 375°F. Grease a 12-cup mini-muffin pan with pan spray or butter. Melt the 4 tablespoons of butter and set aside to cool. With an electric mixer, beat the eggs and agave syrup until the mixture is thick and lemon-colored, about 5 minutes. Add the salt, vanilla, and (cooled) melted butter. With a spatula, stir in the flour and almond meal just until blended. Spoon batter into mini-muffin tin, filling cups halfway. If using berries, place one in each cup at this point, then add a little more batter to each cup. (If no berries are used, fill cups three-quarters full.) Bake 15 minutes. Let cool 5 minutes before removing from pan. Dust with powdered sugar, if desired.

Serves: 12
Prep Time: 10 minutes
Cooking Time: 15 minutes

COCOA-RASPBERRY BABY CAKES

I'm a sucker for individual desserts. Investing in a set of inexpensive ramekins is a great idea. No more "Oh, that's way too big a piece for me."

4 tablespoons butter

2 ounces Trader Joe's Dark Chocolate, chopped

½ cup blanched, slivered almonds

1 cup powdered sugar

¼ cup flour

1 tablespoon cocoa powder

3 egg whites

12 fresh raspberries

powdered sugar for dusting (optional)

VEGETARIAN

Preheat oven to 350°F. Line a 12-cup mini-muffin tin with baking papers. In a saucepan over low heat, melt the butter and chocolate until smooth. Set aside to cool to room temperature. Place the almonds in a food processor and pulse until finely ground. Add the powdered sugar, flour, and cocoa powder, and pulse to combine. Add the cooled butter-and-chocolate mixture and the egg whites, and process to combine. Spoon into the prepared muffin tin, filling each cup half full. Drop a raspberry into each cup. Bake 15 minutes. Cool slightly and dust with additional powered sugar, if desired.

Serves: 12
Prep Time: 10 minutes
Cooking Time: 20 minutes

TART AUX TROIS NOIX

This tart is featured on all holiday dessert tables in our family. Use whatever nuts you love most, and add dried cherries, cranberries, or chopped dried apricots for a chewier texture.

1 Trader Joe's Gourmet Pie Crust (in the frozen-food section), defrosted (refreeze the remaining one for another use)

½ cup bittersweet chocolate, chopped (see note)

8 tablespoons unsalted butter

⅓ cup flavorful honey

2 tablespoons heavy cream

½ cup brown sugar

½ teaspoon vanilla

3 cups (total) hazelnuts, pecans, and walnuts, coarsely chopped

VEGETARIAN

Preheat oven to 375°F. Roll out the pie dough and fit into an 8- or 9-inch pie pan or tart pan with a removable bottom. Cover the pastry with crinkled parchment and weigh it down with a layer of pie weights, raw rice, or dried beans. Place in the oven for 12 minutes. Carefully remove parchment, with weights inside, and return pan to the oven for 5 to 10 minutes, until pastry is dry and golden. Scatter the chopped chocolate over the warm pastry and let sit for a moment, until it begins to melt from the heat of the pastry. Spread the chocolate evenly over the bottom of the pastry shell. In a medium saucepan, combine the butter, honey, cream, and brown sugar and bring to a boil, stirring. Boil 3 to 4 minutes, then stir in nuts and vanilla. Pour into pastry shell and bake 20 minutes.

Serves: 8
Prep Time: 15 minutes
Cooking Time: 45 minutes

I like to use the Pound Plus Bittersweet Chocolate bar—you'll have plenty left over for another purpose (like eating!)

APPENDIX

TECHNIQUES

Since you can't all come to Chez Cherie to learn all the secrets I pass along in my Trader Joe's classes, here's a short course on techniques mentioned in this book, from A to Z. Some of you may already be familiar with these techniques, but you never know, you might pick up some culinary school lore to add a little pizzazz to your cooking!

AL DENTE—The key to perfect pasta, this term means "to the tooth," and describes that a tiny bit of resistance that remains in the noodle after it is properly cooked. Because pasta continues to cook a little bit as you drain it and before it is sauced, when you bite into a piece to check doneness, there should be a tiny bit of tooth resistance. But no crunch! Practice makes perfect here, and pasta practice is never a bad thing!

BREAD CRUMBS FROM SCRATCH—This is the tastiest recycling technique I know. Before the leftover baguette ends or the last focaccia roll sprouts mold, grind them up in a food processor or grate them on a box grater until you've got fluffy crumbs. These have more dimension than the packaged bread crumbs you can buy, and they'll make prettier, crispier toppings for casseroles and gratins. Plus, you'll feel so thrifty when you put the stale bread ends to such tasty use. The crumbs freeze well, so stick them in a plastic bag (recycled, but clean, of course!) and you'll have a frozen stash on hand for any casserole emergency. No need to defrost them—just grab a handful and fluff with your fingers as you scatter away!

CHIFFONADE—Just a chef-y word for thin ribbons, usually of herbs. To make them, stack up a few leaves (of basil, for example) and then roll them, as you would a stack of paper, into a scroll. Starting at one end of the roll, glide your knife through the rolled-up leaves, slicing them into thin ribbons. When you reach the end of the roll, fluff the pile of sliced leaves to separate them. Voila! Pretty and fragrant basil chiffonade, perfect for garnishing many dishes that would benefit from a scattering of tasty green ribbons.

DEGLAZE—This process incorporates all the lovely bits of food that have developed on the bottom of a sauté pan into the sauce. It's usually accomplished by adding a slightly acidic liquid (wine, anyone?) to the pan and stirring gently with a spatula until the bottom of the pan is clean and the flavorful stuff that was lurking there has been loosened. If you prefer to use broth for this rather than wine, a drop or two of lemon juice or vinegar will help the process along. You shouldn't need to scrape the pan with the spatula. Just stir gently after the liquid comes to a simmer and all should be well.

DEVEIN—If your shrimp don't already come deveined, it's a simple process. If the shrimp are already peeled, just stick the tip of a knife under the thin, dark line that extends down the back of the shrimp. Lift the membrane out and discard. If the shrimp have the shell intact, use a thin-bladed knife or kitchen shears to split the shell along the top edge (not where the little fringe-like "legs" are located). Peel the shell off, and then use the technique above to pull the vein out. That little black vein is harmless but it can contain sandy bits that won't complement your saffron crème sauce!

JULIENNE—This technique produces those thin strips or sticks you see in the restaurants without a lot of work. By cutting thick strips of vegetables or meat and then stacking a few of those strips and gliding your chef's knife through them again (the long way), you'll get thinner strips. Need even thinner ones? Just stack and glide again. (Kinda the "lather, rinse, repeat" of the kitchen!) Until your knife skills are rocking, don't make the stacks too high. Better to be safe than get stitches.

RICE 101—If you want to cook rice from scratch rather than using the precooked frozen or shelf-stable rice at TJ's, here's how: You'll need twice as much liquid (water or broth) as you have raw rice. So, to cook a cup of raw rice (which will yield about 3½ cups of cooked rice), you'll want two cups of liquid. In a small saucepan with a tight-fitting lid, bring the liquid to a boil. Stir in the raw rice*, and bring the liquid back to a boil. As soon as you hit that point, give the rice a stir, plop the lid on the pan, and turn the heat down as low as it will go. Simmer, without lifting the lid (that's the key) for fifteen minutes for long grain white rice (like jasmine or basmati) or forty minutes for brown rice. When that time has passed, turn the heat off but *don't lift the lid*. For white rice, you should resist peeking for at least five minutes, and you'll need to wait ten to fifteen minutes for brown rice. This resting period is crucial to producing fluffy, separate grains of rice, but some people have a real problem waiting. (Relax—I promise it's still just rice in there under that lid!) After the resting period, you can fluff the rice, season it, or add "mix-ins" (like chopped nuts or herbs, or sautéed mushrooms) to your heart's content. If the rest of the dinner isn't ready yet, here's a good trick. Place a clean kitchen towel over the top of the pan before you replace the lid. (Gather the corners of the towel up over the top of the lid—you don't want to flambé them accidentally as you finish cooking dinner!) The towel serves as a moisture barrier, which will prevent condensation from forming on the underside of the lid and dripping back down onto the rice, making it sticky.

*A note on rice-rinsing. I don't. I have cooked enough of the rice varieties carried at Trader Joe's over the years that I just don't find it necessary. I've never encountered powdery or dusty rice in all my years of shopping at Joe's. But if you are a confirmed rice-rinser, I have no problem with that. Just be sure to rinse with cold water, because warm or hot water can make the rice sticky. For those unfamiliar with rice-rinsing, some brands of rice are a little powdery in appearance, as if they've been dusted with baby powder. If you encounter rice like this, place the amount you'll be cooking into a strainer (with small holes—otherwise half your rice grains will fall through!) and let cold water run over the rice, moving the grains around with your fingers so all the grains get rinsed. At first, the water that runs out the bottom will appear cloudy. Keep rinsing until the water runs clear and then proceed to cook the rice.

SAUTÉ—Technically, this means to make the food *jump* in the pan, with that impressive arc, like TV chefs do. In our Chez Cherie Basic Cooking series, we encourage students to practice this with a snack-size resealable plastic bag half-full of M&Ms. Once they've mastered the flip (in a room-temperature pan, of course—a hot pan would make this whole thing impossible!), they get to try it with loose candies. Muuuch harder, but I tell them they can eat the ones that jump out! If you want to skip this exercise, you can just use tongs or a spatula to get the food moving in the pan. The main idea is for the food to cook on all sides, so whether flipping, nudging, or turning it over with a spatula, the end result will be the same. I usually prefer a regular pan, not a non-stick pan, for sautéing because the untreated surface seems to heat faster and more evenly, allowing that lovely film of flavor to develop on the bottom of the pan (see *deglaze*).

TOASTING NUTS—While not absolutely essential, I find that toasting nuts creates a wonderful depth of flavor that makes it worth doing. I *always* toast nuts in a sauté pan, *never* in the oven. Why? Because I like to stand at the stove with that sauté pan in one hand (and frequently a glass of wine in the other) and practice my sautéing skills (see *sauté*) for the few moments it takes to make those nuts smell fragrant. That fragrance is the indication that the oil hiding in the nuts has been activated, and the nuts will taste *nuttier* for those few minutes in the pan. Why not the oven? Because if the nuts are in the oven, I'm no longer needed to stand and sauté, which means two things: First, I might miss out on those few sips of wine, because I invariably go off to do something else while the nuts toast away in the oven. Secondly (and possibly more tragically), by the time I smell the toasting nuts and remember that I stashed them in the oven (out of sight, and out of mind until that moment when I smell them), frequently they have, shall we say, "overtoasted"? Yeah, they've burned, and I need to start over, which sometimes means another trip to Joe's. (Not that there's anything wrong with that!)

ZESTING—The outer, colored part of citrus fruit is filled with fabulous flavor and citrus oil. It's rather inconveniently located on top of the bitter-tasting white pith. To remove just the colorful, tasty part—the zest—you'll need a kitchen tool. My very favorite tool for the job is a Microplane zester. These look kind of like a toothy metal ruler, and they remove the zest so efficiently that they would be worth the ten- to twenty-dollar investment even if that were their only use. But they also work wonderfully for grating chocolate, Parmesan cheese, nutmeg, and ginger. I think any well-equipped kitchen should contain one. If you are Microplane-less, a small bartender's tool called a zester will do the job, but you may need to chop the long strands that result. To use either, hold the fruit in your nondominant hand. (I'm a lefty, so the lemon goes in my right hand.) Then, wielding the grater or zester in your other (dominant) hand, run the teeth of the Microplane or the little holed edge of the zester over the surface of the citrus fruit, back and forth, until you have a gloriously fragrant pile of colorful fluff. That's the zest, and you'll be amazed at the flavor impact a pinch of that stuff will have on your food!

HOARDABLES AND PANTRY STAPLES

Here's a list of stuff I like to have on hand at all times—one jar is good, two is better. Some of these items are seasonal, so I'll stock up for the year when they appear on the shelves. Others are just so useful that I like to stockpile them in case of a supply problem or shortage. There's a lot of peace of mind to be had in a well-stocked pantry full of great Trader Joe's products. If you're short on time or energy, you can use the great flavors in these boxes, bags, jars, or containers to whip up easy, fast, and flavorful dishes at a moment's notice without a trip to the store.

ARTISAN PUFF PASTRY *(frozen, seasonal—holiday)*
BALSAMIC VINEGAR
BEEF, VEGETABLE, AND CHICKEN SAVORY BROTH CONCENTRATES
BLACK PEPPER SAUCE
BLACKTHORN FERMENTED CIDER
CALIFORNIA ESTATE OLIVE OIL
CALVADOS *(French apple brandy, seasonal)*
CAPERS IN VINEGAR *(in a jar)*
CHERRIES, DRIED, ESPECIALLY RAINIERS
CHERRY PRESERVES
COCONUT MILK *(canned)*
CORN AND CHILE TOMATO-LESS SALSA
CRANBERRIES, FRESH *(seasonal, in produce aisle—freeze in the bag for use all year)*
CRÈME FRAÎCHE
CRUSHED GINGER *(in a jar)*
FARFALLE PASTA

FROZEN GARLIC CUBES

GENERAL TSAO STIR-FRY SAUCE

GOAT CHEESE *(Trader Joe's Chèvre, Madame Chèvre, or Silver Goat Chèvre)*

GOURMET FRIED ONION PIECES

GRAPESEED OIL

GREEK-STYLE FAGE TOTAL YOGURT

GREEN OLIVE TAPENADE

HARVEST GRAINS BLEND

HATCH VALLEY FIRE-ROASTED DICED GREEN CHILES

HEAVY CREAM

ISRAELI COUSCOUS

JUST ALMOND MEAL

LEMON CURD *(in a jar)*

MAPLE AGAVE SYRUP BLEND

MAPLE SYRUP *(Grade B)*

MASCARPONE

MINI MILK CHOCOLATE PEANUT BUTTER CUPS

MIXED WILD MUSHROOM MEDLEY *(dried)*

NIMAN RANCH APPLEWOOD SMOKED DRY-CURED BACON

ORANGE MUSCAT CHAMPAGNE VINEGAR

ORGANIC POLENTA

ORGANIC PUMPKIN PURÉE *(canned, seasonal—holiday)*

ORGANIC QUINOA

PANCETTA, CHOPPED

PEPITAS *(roasted pumpkin seeds)*

POUND PLUS CHOCOLATE BARS

PROSCIUTTO

PUMPKIN BREAD AND MUFFIN MIX *(seasonal—holiday)*

PUMPKIN BUTTER *(seasonal—holiday)*

RATATOUILLE *(in a jar)*

RED CHILE PEPPER FLAKES

RED WINE VINEGAR

RICE VINEGAR

RICES: BASMATI, JASMINE, ARBORIO, WILD

ROASTED CORN *(frozen)*

SHALLOTS

SOFT LADY FINGERS *(seasonal—holiday)*

SPANISH SAFFRON

SPECK

SPICY, SMOKY PEACH SALSA *(in a jar)*

SWEET CHILI SAUCE

THAI-STYLE RICE STICKS

THAI-STYLE SOY GINGER CARROTS *(frozen)*

TRADER GIOTTO'S PESTO ALLA GENOVESE *(refrigerated)*

TRADER JOE'S GOURMET PIE CRUST *(frozen, seasonal—holiday)*

TURBINADO SUGAR

VERMOUTH, DRY

WHOLE WHEAT COUSCOUS

USEFUL CONVERSIONS

1 teaspoon	5 milliliters
1 tablespoon	15 milliliters
1 cup	240 milliliters
1 pint (2 cups)	470 milliliters
1 quart (4 cups)	.95 liter
1 gallon (4 quarts)	3.8 liters
1 fluid ounce	30 milliliters/28 grams
1 ounce	28 grams
1 pound (16 ounces)	454 grams
350°F / 400°F	175°C / 200°C

RECIPE INDEX

A

A Meal on Its Own Pasta, 150
All-About-TJ's Salad, 35
Almond-Agave Baby Cakes, 204
Almond-Plum Galette, 193
Almost-from-Scratch Butternut Squash Soup with
    Bourbon, 53
Apple Sausage and Cheddar Bites, 20
Artichoke and Basil Spread, 17
Arugula, Chicken, and Walnut Salad, 45
Asian Flavors Slaw, 39
Asian-Flavored Pork, 114
Asian-Style Chicken with Sesame Nuts, 86
Asparagus Tart, 24
Asparagus, Provolone, and Prosciutto Involtini, 19
Autumn Squash with Chili Flavors, 170
Avocado, Orange, and Olive Salad, 37

B

Baked Camembert with Honey and Hazelnuts, 18
BBQ Pasta Salad, 152
Berry-Zin Sauce, 185
Best Pasta Kevin Ever Had, 153
Better-than-Tiramisu, 187
Black Bean Salad, 61
Black Pepper Chicken with Winter Squash, 79
Blackberry Fool, 180
Bourbon-Balsamic Beef, 97
Bread Pudding with Bourbon Sauce, 190
Brenna's Nutty and Wild Rice Salad, 65
Brie and Pear Galette, 26
Burgundy Lamb and Cipollini, 104

C

Caramelized Onion, Fig, and Gorgonzola Tart, 27
Carne Asada Salad, 40
Champagne Chicken with Champignons, 83
Champagne-Saffron Risotto, 73
Cherry Crostini with Pecorino Romano, 13
Cherry Pork with a Kick, 116
Cherry Rice Pilaf, 69
Cherry-Berry Crisp, 191
Chicken and Peppers in Crème Sauce, 84

Chicken with Olives, 87
Chile and Crab Chowder, 57
Chipotle Flat Iron Steak Salad with Roasted Baby
    Artichokes, 96–97
Chocolate Pumpkin Tart, 199
Citrus and Harvest Grains Salad, 68
Cocoa-Raspberry Baby Cakes, 205
Compound Butters for Steak, 102
Corn and Basil Rice, 63
Couscous with Dried Fruit, 66
Cranberry Pork, 119
Crayon-Box Tomato and Candied Nut Salad, 33
Cream of Chicken Soup with Wild Rice, 55
Creamy Tomato and Roasted Red Pepper Soup with
    Pesto Gnocchi, 50

D

Double Blackberry Tart, 189

E

End of the Season Green Bean Salad, 177

F

Farfalle with Green Beans and Feta, 141
Fat Tire Flammade, 101
Fettuccine with Shrimp and Saffron Crème, 155
Frat Brats, 108

G

Gambas y Jambon, 132
General Tsao Chicken Wraps, 80
General Tsao Pork with Rice Sticks, 120
Gingerbread with Mascarpone and Pears, 186
Glamour Salmon, 136
Gorgonzola Fusilli, 147
Gourmet Magazine-Inspired Ham Cups, 107
Green Bean, Tomato, and Olive Salad, 37
Green Beans with Cambozola Sauce, 160
Green Beans with Mushroom Brie, 174
Green Beans with Red Onion and Creamy Feta
    Dressing, 158
Green Olive and Gorgonzola Palmiers, 21
Grilled Flatbread Salad, 44

H

Hairdresser Blondies, 183
Hazelnut-Plum Baby Cakes, 203
Hearty Sherried Mushroom Soup, 54
Hot Toddy Chicken, 80

I

Israeli Couscous, 67

K

Kevin's Favorite Pumpkin Black Bean Soup, 58

L

Lamb Loin with Pomegranate Reduction, 103
Lemon-Vodka Pasta, 142
Linguini with Leeks, Shrimp, and Arugula, 144
Lotsa Lemon Pasta, 151

M

Maple Balsamic Pork Chops, 113
Maple Mustard Chicken, 88
Margarita Pork Chops, 121
Margarita Shrimp, 133
Marsala-Roasted Pork, 113
Mashed Sweet Potatoes, 173
Matt's Magic Mushrooms, 16
Maui Beef on Coconut Rice with Macadamia Nuts and Basil, 94
Maxi-Mini Peanut Butter Cup Cookies, 200
Meatball Spiedini with Ovolini, 23
Meyer Lemon Raspberry Clouds, 198
Mini Vanilla Wafer Cheesecakes, 194
Mushroom Hazelnut Rice, 66
Mushroom Marsala Sauce, 169

N

Nectarine, Gorgonzola, and Greens, 30

O

Olive Butterflies, 139
One-Pot Pesto Pasta, Potatoes, and Green Beans, 149

P

Pappa al Pomodoro Ricco, 51
Pasta Mollica, 140
Pasta Provençal, 146
Pasta with Pumpkin Sauce, 143
Pecan Green Beans, 175
Peppered Beef and Rice Sticks, 95
Perline Pasta, Prosciutto, and Pea Soup, 49
Pesto Chicken Salad, 81
Pesto Pork, 110
Pork and Peppers, 115
Pork with Cider, 116
Pork with Dried Cranberries and Pine Nuts, 123
Pork with Vermouth, 111
Potato-Kale Minestra, 56
Potsticker Soup, 52
Prosciutto Turkey Tenderloin with Fingerlings, 82
Prosciutto-Wrapped Chicken, 89
Puff Pastry Pillows, 196
Pumpkin and Carnitas Salad, 43
Pumpkin Cranberry Cake with Pumpkin Butter–
    Mascarpone Slather, 201

Q

Quick Almond Cake, 202
Quick Black Beans and Rice, 64
Quinoa with Grilled Vegetables and Mini-Peppers, 69
Quinoa-Stuffed Grilled Mushrooms, 70

R

Raspberry Caramel Turnovers, 182
Red Wine Pasta, 154
Red, White, and Blue Firecracker Potato Salad, 74
Roasted Apricots with Honeyed Goat Cheese, 14
Roasted Asparagus with Hazelnuts and Clementines,
    163
Roasted Butternut Squash with Pecans, Dried
    Cherries, and Blue Cheese, 166

Roasted Mushroom Polenta Stacks, 71
Roasted Pear, Prosciutto, and Goat Cheese Parcels, 22
Roasted Potatoes, Shrimp, and Pancetta, 130
Roasted Pumpkin and Green Beans with Prosciutto and Parmesan, 167
Roasted Zucchini and Mushrooms with Pesto, 160

S

Saffron Potatoes and Pancetta, 74
Sassy Peach Sweet Potatoes, 172
Sausage and Spuds Salad, 42
Sausage Salad for a Hot Summer Night, 41
Sautéed Chard of Many Colors with Pine Nuts, 161
Scalloped Corn, 176
Shrimp in Hard Cider, 129
Shrimp on Polenta Pillows, 128
Silky, Sinful Chocolate Tart, 184
Sirloin Salad with a Latin Kick, 100
South of France Halibut, 136
Southern Greens with Pancetta and White Beans, 168
Spanish-Style Pork, 117
Spicy Apricot-Glazed Pork, 122
Spicy Corny Green Beans, 172
Steak and Green Bean Salad with Blue Cheese, 99
Sugar Snap Peas, Corn, and Bacon with Basil Butter, 164
Sweet Potato, Pecan, and Cranberry Salad, 32
Sweet-Glazed Salmon with Corn Salsa, 134

T

Tart aux Trois Noix, 206
Thai Beef Salad, 100
Thai Ginger Carrots with Shrimp and Green Beans, 127
Thanksgiving in a Bowl, 52
These Little Piggies, 17
TJ's Trifle, 188
Tri-Tip Asada with Heirloom Tomatoes, 92
Tsao Nuts, 15
Tumble-Fruit Crumble, 195
Turkey with Green Chile Sauce, 78

V

Vigneron's Sausages (The Winemaker's Sausages), 112

W

Warm Almonds and Olives, 11
Warm Mushroom Salad, 38
Wild Rice with Shiitakes, 64
Winter Holiday Salad, 34

Y

Ya Ya Cherie's Quick and Dirty Jambalaya, 72

INGREDIENT INDEX

A

Ace pear cider, 129
All Natural Barbecue Sauce
Almondina cookies, 100
Artisan Puff Pastry, 20, 24, 27, 182, 196
Artisan Style Whole Grain Loaf, 13, 140

B

Baby Beets, 35
Baby Spring Mix, 44, 100
BBQ Shredded Pork, 17
Black Angus Steak Tips, 101
Black Pepper Sauce, 79
Blackberry Preserves, 189
Blackthorn Fermented Cider, 78, 116, 129
Blue Agave Sweetener. See Organic Blue Agave
    Sweetener
Bold and Smoky Kansas City-Style Barbecue Sauce,
    74, 152
Burgundy Pepper Lamb Tips, 104
Burrata cheese, 153
Butcher Shop Bone-In Frenched Center-Cut Pork
    Chops, 121
Butcher Shop Natural Boneless Pork Loin Chops, 113,
    122
Butternut Squash Soup, 52
Butternut Apple Soup, 52

C

Cannellini (White Kidney Beans), 168
Capers in Vinegar, 146
Carne Asada Autentica, 40, 92
Chard of Many Colors, 56, 150, 161
Cherry Preserves, 13, 116
Chèvre, 14, 35, 139, 149, 150, 177
Chili Pepper Hot Sauce, 14, 57, 116, 132, 143, 173
Ciliegine mozzarella, 23
Corn and Chile Tomato-Less Salsa, 40, 70, 100, 108,
    134, 152, 164, 172
Crushed Ginger, 39, 86, 97, 114, 134
Artisan Style Whole Grain Loaf, 13, 140

D

Dark Chocolate bars, 184, 205
Dark Chocolate Covered Caramels, 182
Dark Chocolate Stars, 199
Deep, Dark Gingerbread and Baking Mix, 186

E

Eggplant Garlic Spread, 21

F

Fancy Berry Medley, 185
Fancy Shredded Mexican Blend, 170
Fat Tire beer, 101
Flat Iron Beef Chuck Steak Seasoned in a Chipotle
    Pepper BBQ Sauce, 96

Fresh Apricot Preserves, 122, 196
Fresh Raspberry Preserves, 182, 202

G

General Tsao Stir-Fry Sauce, 80, 114, 120
Genova Pesto, 81, 107, 110, 149, 160
Golden Berry Blend, 190
Gourmet Fried Onion Pieces, 52, 174
Gourmet Pie Crust, 26, 184, 189, 193, 199, 206
Greek Olive Medley, 11
Green Olive Tapenade, 21, 139, 146
Grilled Vegetable Bruschetta, 69

H

Haricots Verts (French green beans), 33, 41, 120
Harvest Grains Blend, 68
Hatch Valley Fire-Roasted Diced Green Chiles, 78, 170
Hawaiian Style Maui Beef Boneless Short Ribs, 84
Herb Salad Mix, 32, 38, 40, 41, 44
Hofbrau Brats, 108
Hot and Sweet Sesame Nuts, 86

I

Israeli Couscous, 67

J

Jack's Catch Premium Crab, 57
Jalapeño Pepper Hot Sauce, 14, 57, 116, 132, 143, 173
Julienned Sun-Dried Tomatoes, 128
Just Almond Meal, 202
Just Chicken, 44, 72, 81, 204

L

Lean Beef Stew Meat, 101
Lemon Curd, 187

M

MacTarnahan's Oregon Honey Beer, 108
Maple Agave Syrup Blend, 41
Mediterranean Cheese Style Yogurt, 196
Mexican Blend cheese, 170
Mini Milk Chocolate Peanut Butter Cups, 200
Minisweet Bell Peppers, 69, 84, 115, 152

Mixed Medley Cherry Tomatoes, 23, 33, 37, 40, 44, 152
Mixed Wild Mushroom Medley, 54, 113, 169
Multigrain Baking and Pancake Mix, 183

N

Niman Ranch Applewood Smoked Dry-Cured Bacon, 16, 147, 150, 164
Niman Ranch Applewood Smoked Cured Black Forest Ham, 107

O

Orange Muscat Champagne Vinegar, 34, 35, 41, 61, 68
Organic Blue Agave Sweetener, 134, 195, 204
Organic Polenta, 71, 128
Organic Pumpkin Purée, 143
Organic Spaghetti, 154
Organic Vodka Pasta Sauce, 23
Ovolini mozzarella, 23

P

Party Size Mini Meatballs, 23
Perline Pasta and Prosciutto, 49
Pesto alla Genovese, 50, 81, 107, 110, 149, 160
Pizza Dough, 44
Polenta. See Organic Polenta
Potato Medley, 57, 74
Pound Plus Bittersweet Chocolate bar, 206
Pumpkin Bread and Muffin Mix, 201
Pumpkin Butter, 199
Pumpkin Purée. See Organic Pumpkin Purée

Q

Quattro Formaggio, 100
Quinoa, 69, 70

R

Ratatouille, 136
Red Pepper Spread with Eggplant and Garlic, 21
Ricotta cheese, 153
Rice Sticks, 95, 120
Roasted Red Pepper and Artichoke Tapenade, 21, 50, 139
Roasted Vegetable Tapenade, 100
Rustico Pomodoro Pasta Sauce, 71